The
Seven Deadly
SKILLS of
Communicating

The

Seven Deadly

SKILLS of

Communicating

Ros Jay

INTERNATIONAL THOMSON BUSINESS PRESS
I(T)P® An International Thomson Publishing Company

London • Bonn • Johannesburg • Madrid • Melbourne • Mexico City • New York • Paris
Singapore • Tokyo • Toronto • Albany, NY • Belmont, CA • Cincinnati, OH • Detroit, MI

The Seven Deadly Skills of Communicating

Copyright © 1999 Ros Jay

I(T)P® A division of International Thomson Publishing Inc.
The ITP logo is a trademark under licence

British Library Cataloguing-in-Publication Data
A catalogue record for this book in available from the British Library

First edition published 1999 by International Thomson Business Press

Typeset by J&L Composition Ltd, Filey, North Yorkshire
Printed in the UK by TJ International, Padstow, Cornwall

ISBN 1–86152–373–4

International Thomson Business Press
Berkshire House
168–173 High Holborn
London WC1V 7AA
UK

http://www.itbp.com

Contents

Introduction

You can't avoid communicating with your staff; even when you're not speaking directly to them, you're sending out unconscious messages. For example, every time you keep some piece of information secret you send your employees a message that you don't trust them with it. Poor communication in a company or a department leads to low morale and a negative attitude from the staff. This in turn leads to low productivity and high staff turnover. It is equally important to be able to communicate effectively with senior management, in order to convince them to provide what your department needs to be successful and motivated.

But it's perfectly possible to take control of the deliberate and subliminal messages you communicate to other people in the organization. By communicating the right information, and choosing the right medium to do it, you can generate an atmosphere in which employees are happier, better motivated and more productive. This will be a positive stimulant for your department or company and will make your own job as a manager easier and more rewarding – not to mention, of course, reflecting well on your management skills.

This book examines the seven core skills of good communication throughout the organization, which between them will ensure productive and motivated staff at every level:

1   developing a corporate personality;

2   written communication;

3   verbal communication;

4   communicating with senior management;

5   communicating with the team;

6   communicating with the individual;

7   communicating under pressure.

Why communication matters

Does it really make much difference how you communicate with your staff? If you were to put into practice all the techniques in this book, would you notice any change? The answer is a definite yes. Staff loyalty and motivation, and therefore productivity, would significantly increase. Good communication benefits everyone involved:

➤ *The organization.* Good communication produces a well motivated and productive staff. This in turn leads to increased loyalty and lower staff turnover.

➤ *The manager.* When information is flowing freely between departmental managers and senior management, it is far easier for managers to work effectively because they can get their point across and can generate the support they need. Equally, when managers understand the views and feelings of their teams, they are better equipped to help them work to their full potential.

➤ *The department or team.* A team which has easy access to all the information which affects it can work much more effectively and can anticipate the changes it needs to make to fit in with what is going on in the rest of the organization.

➤ *The individual staff.* People who are kept informed, and asked for their opinions and views, feel that the management trusts them and considers them important. The corollary of this is that if you keep people in the dark they will assume that you don't care how they feel. Good communication leads to better motivated and more loyal staff, who enjoy their work more, like the organization they work for and stay with it for longer.

The word 'communication' comes from the Latin word for 'to share'. One of the recurring themes of good communication is that it must be shared, or two-way, to be effective. Good communication is as much about listening as it is about speaking. It doesn't matter how much information you give your staff, or how effectively you impart it; if they can't respond you haven't got a communication system going, merely an information channel. There is a classic description of large organizations with poor communication, which is that information travels upwards through a series of filters, and instructions travel downwards through a series of loud hailers.

People must be able to reply, to comment and to give you information freely. This will make them feel they have an input, and therefore a stake, in whatever is going on. This contribution to the decision-making process gives people a shared responsibility for the decisions which are generated. And if people accept responsibility for a decision, they are more committed and more motivated to see it through.

What do you want to say?

Before you can communicate you have to have something to say. So what kind of information should you be giving your staff? And won't they find out sooner or later anyway? If you don't tell your staff what's going on, they'll make it up for themselves: that's human nature. And the chances are they'll make up something far more dramatic, scandalous or frightening than the simple truth that you're keeping from them. It's secrecy that fertilizes the company grapevine. Some information is, of course, genuinely confidential. But even allowing for this, virtually all companies tell their staff too little rather than too much.

Rumour is the key. There is only one way to contain rumours and that is to tell your staff everything they are interested in so there is no room for them to speculate. They know exactly whether or not the company is planning to move to new premises because you've told them – so what's there to spread rumours about? You may not be able to stop them gossiping about whether the accounts manager is pregnant or just putting on weight, but you can stop them spreading damaging stories about important changes or developments in the organization.

If you want to know what your staff are interested in, again, what do they spread rumours about? If the subject in question is one they discuss between themselves, or would if they knew it was an issue, they clearly want to know about it. So your default setting should be to tell your staff everything. There are two exceptions to this rule: information that is genuinely confidential and information that is too insignificant to waste time on.

Information that is genuinely confidential

Of course there are some things you really can't tell staff, but most organizations extend this rule much too far. Suppose you're considering expanding into new premises; this is the kind of information many companies would try to keep quiet until the new premises were found and most of the decisions about which departments would be moved had been taken. But why? Why not tell your staff that you have made the decision to expand and you're currently looking for a good location? Tell them what you haven't decided – so they won't speculate that you have but aren't saying anything. Tell them that you hope to move in between six and twelve months from now, and that which departments move will depend on the premises.

Let them ask questions – this will tell you a lot about what issues matter to them, which is all useful information for you when it comes to choosing a new site. Perhaps they care a lot about how nearby it is, or whether you are looking for something with better facilities or simply more space. Or perhaps they are concerned that customer services and accounts should both be in the same place. If these factors affect motivation, you should know about them now. But if you try to keep the whole matter secret you will never be able to acquire this information – and you'll fail at keeping the secret as well.

Having said all that, some things are obviously not for general consumption. These things fall into two categories: personal and commercial information. Personal confidences include the fact that a certain member of staff is gay, having a nervous breakdown, or not really on holiday but having an abortion. Clearly you don't pass on this sort of information. Commercial confidences are those that would damage the business if they got out to customers or competitors.

But make sure you can come up with a good reason for not telling the staff, or not telling them yet. And if possible, give them some information and tell them why you can't give them the rest. Suppose you are planning to launch a new product line ahead of your competitors, and there's a lot of secret planning of launch events and reorganizing production schedules going on. The staff are bound to realize something's up. So admit it. The key rule is: if they're going to hear it somewhere – press, customers, rumour or anywhere else – make sure they hear it from you first. If information is supposed to be confidential, make sure it's so confidential there aren't even any rumours going around. Once the rumours start, tell the staff as much as you can. For example:

> We have an exciting new product, which will knock our competitors for six, but they mustn't find out about it until we launch. We'd love to tell you all about it, but if the information somehow reached our competitors it could knock our profits badly. What's more, you would all theoretically fall under suspicion for leaking the information, and that wouldn't be fair on you. So we're only telling the people that are involved for the moment, but we will let you in on the secret as soon as we feel we can.

Information that is too insignificant to waste time on

It's all very well saying tell your staff everything, but you'd never get any other work done if you discussed every tiny point with them. You should tell your staff everything which affects them and their work, and remember that they can be affected psychologically as well. If you are laying off staff in another department, it may not affect your own section's work directly, but it is bound to make them wonder whether they are next. You may not think it significant, because you know they will be unaffected, but they don't know that until you tell them.

You will benefit in many ways from telling your staff as much as possible. We've already seen that it increases motivation and loyalty and therefore productivity. And it will reduce staff turnover. It also helps to prevent rumours. Another advantage is that the more you tell your staff, the less likely they are to believe any rumours they hear. If someone says 'Hey! Guess what I've just heard. There's a firm of management consultants coming in and apparently they're going to be asked to recommend a departmental reshuffle,' the likely response will be 'Nonsense. We'd have been told if that was the case.' If your staff trust you to tell them everything you reasonably can, they will view less reliable information with the scepticism it deserves. If your staff believe every bit of dubious gossip going round, you have only yourself to blame.

It also follows that you should be giving out information as early as you can. Someone somewhere will have been asked to type a letter to the management consultants, for example, so the information that they are being called in is going to circulate whatever you do. The first question everyone will want answered is 'Why?' So make sure you give them the answer before they make it up for themselves.

The other important rule is that you should never lie to your staff: this is tantamount to crying wolf. Why should they ever believe you again? And information your staff don't believe is worth less than no information at all. People's memories are long. Suppose you tell them that low profits aren't going to mean job cuts and then six months later you cut jobs. They won't have forgotten it five years later when you tell them that this year's poor profits won't mean redundancies – and they won't believe you. Instead, they'll ignore your remarks and continue to gossip and become demoralized.

Summary

Good communication is essential for everyone in the organization and leads to:

➢ less gossip;

➢ better motivation;

➢ higher productivity;

➢ increased staff loyalty;

➢ lower staff turnover.

You should tell your staff everything which affects them or their work, except for:

1 information that genuinely must be kept confidential;

2 information that is too insignificant – to your staff as well as to you – to waste time on.

When you communicate information to your staff you should:

➢ tell them as much as you can;

➢ tell them as soon as you can;

➢ never lie to them.

1

The First Deadly Skill

Developing a Corporate Personality

Every organization has a corporate personality. This is most often discussed in the context of its external corporate image, but its internal image is equally important. It is bound to be related to the public image, but it won't be exactly the same.

Whether you like it or not, your organization has characteristics that its staff are well aware of: they may see it as being uncaring, friendly, formal, modern, easy-going, domineering, or as having any number of other 'human' personality traits. This chapter will examine:

➤ what is a corporate personality?

➤ how to identify your own corporate personality;

➤ how to change your personality from the one you have to the one you want.

Part of this process may well involve taking a closer look at the organization's mission statement, so this chapter will also look at what mission statements are all about and how to draw one up.

What is a corporate personality?

Your corporate personality is a reflection of the personalities of the people who work within the organization. Of course people are all different, as you may rightly argue, but the people in your organization will all possess certain common traits which are strengthened by belonging to an organization which exhibits those same traits.

Let me give you an example. Imagine an organization which is, corporately, unhelpful and obstructive. Whenever a manager asks a fellow manager for co-operation, it always seems to be more of a fight than it should be to get them to help. If one of the staff asks someone from another department to supply some urgent information, it somehow takes ages and they have to be asked at least four times. And you can bet, in an organization like this, that if anyone asks one of the directors for support, it is rarely forthcoming – at least not willingly.

Now suppose you get a job as a senior manager for this organization. You've been charged with overseeing a lot of developments in your departments, and you're excited and enthusiastic about the job. You need to ask a couple of the directors for advice – but they are difficult to track down and can't fit in a meeting with you for another five weeks. You ask the accounts department to let you have the figures for your departments' budgets and expenditure over the last three years; somehow, after three weeks and endless phone calls, they still haven't materialized. You ask some of your junior managers to prepare proposals for forthcoming developments in time for a meeting on Friday week. None of them turns up on time for the meeting and most of them so far have only cobbled together a few notes. And so it goes on.

What do you do about this apathy and unhelpfulness? Within a few months most people do one of two things: they start working in the same way as everyone else, on the basis that it may not be good for the organization but it makes their own lives a good deal easier, or they leave. Obstructiveness and apathy may not be their natural working style, but the people who choose to stay will possess a capability for it – which is why the corporate personality will be a reflection of the people who work within it.

So which came first, the chicken or the egg? Is the organization a reflection of its people, or are they a reflection of it? In a way, it doesn't really matter. The fact is that organizations like this get better and better at employing apathetic and obstructive people in the first place – it keeps staff turnover down, after all. Organizations which are a constant hotbed of conflict and back-stabbing can spot a non-team player at a hundred paces, and offer them a job. Organizations which are domineering and obsessively hierarchical employ submissive and unenterprising people. And, likewise, organizations which are helpful, friendly and co-operative can identify their own kind when they are recruiting.

The one thing which is certain, however, is that corporate personality, however it is created, is perpetuated from the top. If the directors on the board are unhelpful, secretive, hierarchical or uncaring, you can be sure that everyone else will follow suit or get out. If the corporate personality is a negative one, the responsibility for it must lie with the directors and senior management. They have the power to change the working style of their organization and their influence will filter down to everyone given time.

I can give you a fascinating example of this. In the 1960s and 1970s the Chairman of the National Coal Board, Alf Robens (later Lord Robens), used to visit coal pits around the country and talk to the management. He was surprised to find that often, when he visited two pits only a few miles apart, the staff at one would be obstructive and bloody-minded, while the employees at the other pit would be co-operative and reasonable.

It took him a long time to find the reason, but eventually he worked it out: it was always determined by the personality of the original pit owner back in the 19th century. The ones who treated their people badly had bred a culture of mistrust and resistance to management in their pits which had passed from generation to generation. Meanwhile, the popular pit owners had generated a culture of co-operation and understanding among their staff.

Internal and external image

Your corporate personality as it is perceived within the organization is not necessarily the same thing as your external personality, which is an aspect of your corporate image. However, it stands to reason that if a particular attitude is prevalent in the way that people deal with each other, this attitude is likely to spill over into the way they deal with outsiders: advisers, suppliers, job applicants and – crucially – customers.

If you treat your staff as though they are important, they are far more likely to give the same kind of respect to your customers. If, on the other hand, you treat your staff dismissively, they will undoubtedly pass this treatment on. Apart from anything else, they couldn't care less if the customer never comes back. That will only damage the organization which treats them so badly, which seems like deserved revenge from your staff's point of view.

Your internal corporate personality may not be exactly the same as your external image, but it won't be very different. You can't maintain a reputation for being caring to your customers for very long if you treat your staff as if they didn't matter to you; sooner or later your own employees will undermine your public reputation. An internal reputation for obstructiveness may be converted into an external image of apathy rather than deliberate unhelpfulness, but a negative internal trait will always manifest itself as a similar negative trait externally.

It should be clear from this that your external personality follows on from your internal one, and not the other way round. This means that you cannot successfully correct a poor public image without simultaneously working on your internal personality. On the other hand, if you can create a strong, positive internal image, you will find – once it has had time to filter through – that this process does most of the work of correcting your external image for you as well.

How to identify your own corporate personality

In order to ensure your personality traits are positive ones, you need to identify them. This really shouldn't be too difficult in principle; most people at any level in an organization know perfectly well what the basic corporate personality is. Usually they are on the receiving end of it, whether it is good or bad. But if you really want to improve your image with your own employees, it's worth finding out quite specifically what they think of you. And there's a very easy way to do this: you ask them.

By far the simplest and most effective method of identifying your corporate personality is to survey your staff. Ask them what traits they associate with the organization and what traits they would like to see. This is very straightforward, and we'll look at an example of a survey form in a moment, but there are a few points to bear in mind when you carry out this exercise:

➢   People will not be honest with you unless they are confident that the survey is entirely anonymous, and that they won't – and can't – be identified if they make any negative criticisms.

Not only should the survey forms be unnamed, they should also ask respondents to tick boxes so they don't worry that their handwriting will be identified. Give people the option of adding comments at the end, but make sure the survey is useful even if they don't. Distribute survey sheets randomly, or let people help themselves from a pile, so they don't think you have coded each form so as to identify the respondent later (yes, some organizations generate this level of paranoia in their staff).

➤ The less positive your image, the less loyalty your staff will feel towards you. Why should they help you by filling in your stupid form, they will think, what have you ever done for them? If your image is poor, so will the response to the survey be. You should, therefore, be worried by a low response. However, you should do everything you can to generate a high response, other than make it compulsory (the kind of organization which forces its employees to respond to this kind of survey is not in the frame of mind to start making improvements in its staff relations). You should explain on the form why it is in people's interests to complete it: so that you can improve their working environment. And you should convince them you will really respond to the survey by telling them verbally that this is an important survey, and you are planning big changes but you need their help in letting you know what precisely needs to change.

➤ Survey absolutely everyone, from senior management downwards (and be sure you don't omit anyone such as delivery drivers who are almost never on site, or two people based in an outlying office somewhere). Managers may feel more bound to be loyal – even on an anonymous survey – than their staff will. So tell your managers that you want honesty, not loyalty.

➤ If your organization is large, it may consist of several very separate departments, perhaps in different locations. You may even have branches all over the country. Analyse the surveys from each of these separately, because any significant differences could be important. If you have 17 branches, 15 with mostly negative images among their staff and two with positive responses to the survey, it looks as if two of your branch managers could teach you (and the other 15) a good deal. You won't know this if you analyse all the responses in one lump. However, don't analyse very small groups or departments separately because people feel safer responding if they know their comments are not only anonymous, but also hidden in amongst a large group of responses; there's safety in numbers. If a department of three or four all respond with negative comments, and you analyse them as a group of three, you'll know more than they want you to about who said what. In any case, the larger the sample the more accurate the results.

➤ Let people know when you will have analysed the results of the survey and promise to give them a summary of the results. And do it. Be honest about any criticisms generated, and absolutely don't attempt to justify yourselves.

➤ If you are not seen to make a positive improvement as a direct result of this survey, you will undermine staff morale far more than if you had never run the survey. It is a cardinal rule of corporate communication that lies, broken promises and unfulfilled expectations have a vastly more damaging effect on the organization than no comment, no promises and no expectations.

The survey form

The survey form itself should be very simple. It should start with a brief explanation of what it is for, why it is worth filling it in and what you will do as a result of the survey. Then simply print a list of personality traits and ask people to tick all those which they associate with the organization. It can help to give them two columns to tick: ask them to tick the three which they feel best describe the organization in the first column, and any others which they think also apply in the second column.

List the words randomly to avoid leading people in any particular direction; in the example below they are listed alphabetically, which creates as random a mix of positive and negative words as anything else would.

Below this section, produce another list of words – positive ones – and ask respondents to choose the three qualities which they consider most important in the organization. Then include a space in which people are invited to make additional comments if they want to. And that's it. Simple to produce, quick to fill in and easy to analyse. Here's an example:

STAFF SURVEY

What sort of organization do you work for?

We'd be very grateful if you'd find a few moments to fill in this survey form. It's important that you feel happy working with us and that you like the organization. There's always room for improvement, and that's where you come in. We want to do everything we can to improve our relationship with you, but we need your help. There are two things we need to know from you: how do you see the organization now and how would you like to see it?

The more of you who return this form to us, the better chance we have of creating the best environment for all of us. As you can see, the survey is anonymous; we hope this will encourage you all to be honest, which is what we want. We plan to have your responses analysed by the end of October and we'll let you know the results. After that, we will implement any changes necessary to bring the style and personality of the organization closer to what you want.

How to fill in the survey

Below is a list of words with two columns of boxes beside them. In the first column, please tick the three words which you feel best describe this organization. In the second column, please tick any other words which you think also apply.

	Tick 3	Tick any
aggressive		
ambitious		
apathetic		
back-stabbing		
bureaucratic		
businesslike		
caring		
co-operative		
dictatorial		
dishonest		
dynamic		

easy-going		
efficient		
enthusiastic		
exciting		
formal		
friendly		
frustrating		
hardworking		
helpful		
hierarchical		
honest		
kind		
lazy		
modern		
negative		
obstructive		
open		
overbearing		
perfectionist		
picky		
positive		
respectful		
secretive		
staid		
strict		
stuffy		
supportive		
tough		
underhand		
unhelpful		
weak		
welcoming		

Please tick the three words on the list below which best describe the kind of organization you would like this to be.

	Tick 3
ambitious	
businesslike	
caring	
co-operative	
dynamic	
easy-going	
efficient	
enthusiastic	
exciting	
formal	
friendly	
hardworking	
helpful	
hierarchical	
honest	
kind	
modern	
open	
perfectionist	
positive	
respectful	
strict	
supportive	
tough	
welcoming	

Please add any other comments in the box below if you wish.

Many thanks for helping us by filling in this survey. Please post it in the box provided at reception when you have completed it.

What corporate personality would you prefer?

Once you have analysed the results of your survey, it should be clear where you are and where you need to get to. It is very rare for an organization to produce wildly differing results, except perhaps in entirely different sections of the company. If half your staff think the organization is apathetic, lazy and obstructive, the other half are unlikely to think it dynamic, enthusiastic and co-operative. They might describe it as bureaucratic, frustrating and unhelpful, which is less damning but clearly symptomatic of the same general ailment.

If your employees basically like the organization but find it frustrating at times, they are likely to choose less negative words – such as 'unhelpful' rather than 'obstructive'. If the survey results show up a lot of harsh words such as 'apathetic' (where 'lazy' might have done), or 'picky' (rather than 'perfectionist') it is likely that your staff really don't like 'the organization'.

So you can see what your current image is with your staff. The next question is, what would you like it to be? This is where the second half of the survey comes in. People aren't stupid. They are not likely to choose words which simply don't suit the organization. They are realistic and if they wanted to work for a 'dynamic, enthusiastic, ambitious' organization, they wouldn't have joined a traditional clockmaker. You should find that the words most often picked from the second list are perfectly commensurate with the kind of business you are running.

If what your staff would really like is to work for a 'kind, caring, friendly' organization, then why shouldn't they? The object of the exercise here is to create as happy a staff as possible for all the reasons we saw earlier – to boost morale, motivation and productivity, and to reduce staff turnover. So give them what they want, for goodness' sake.

There is a reason for asking people to tick only three options in the second question. It makes it easier to produce only three clear 'winners' when you come to analyse the full set of responses. And you really need a maximum of three final words because you are going to have to focus clearly on these personality traits. Too many and you would lose clarity of purpose in implementing the next stage of the process.

Changing your corporate personality

Overhauling your corporate personality is relatively simple. It isn't easy, though. It takes a lot of hard work and commitment from the top, but if you are prepared to make the effort, you can do it. There is one crucial factor above all else, however: it must come from the top and from everyone at the top. People follow the example they are set and it's no good if only some of the directors play ball. One part-time director with the old, negative approach can do a huge amount of damage, so it's imperative that the entire board of directors are behind the initiative and recognize that they *are*, in effect, the organization; if the organization is to change, they must change.

And that is the crux of it: it's all to do with people. If the collective attitudes of the people in the organization change, the corporate personality will change too. So the attitude of the directors and senior management must change, and it is the job of those managers to make sure that the managers under them adopt the new attitude as well, once the example has been set.

It's no good ordering managers to behave differently – that kind of approach directly contradicts the new, positive attitude. You must persuade and convince them that attitudes need to change, show them how to do it and then support them in their efforts.

Using the key words

So what precisely are you changing your corporate personality to? This is where your three key words come in. You need to focus on the key qualities which your employees chose when you surveyed them. Perhaps they indicated that they would like the organization to come across as 'kind, caring and friendly'. So focus on these attitudes. Ask each manager to do two things:

➤ They should come up with at least three initiatives to implement within the next two months which will promote this attitude. They might propose a monthly departmental lunch – perhaps even a lunch with another department they work closely with. Maybe they will adopt a policy of allowing staff to choose whether they want to start their eight-hour day at 9.00 or 9.30, as a help to those employees with children to be dropped at school. These initiatives should not be a one-off event and then everything's back to normal. They should be regular events or permanent policies. Give each manager a budget; it doesn't have to be a lot and the return in improved morale should be more than worth it. A monthly lunch, for example, only needs to consist of some good quality sandwiches and a couple of bottles of wine. A flexitime arrangement costs nothing.

➤ The initiatives should relate to your three key words. If the staff had proposed the words 'exciting, dynamic and ambitious' you would expect to see different initiatives – perhaps regular visits for all staff to trade shows to see the latest products in their field, or support and help in training or qualifications for people who want it.

➤ Each manager should also consider the key focus words before any significant interaction with employees. Before writing a memo, holding an appraisal interview or running a team meeting, they should stop to make a mental check that they are doing it in a way which reflects the new corporate approach. Are memos worded appropriately? Are employees being given a chance to prepare properly? Is the room set up suitably – are you facing your appraisee across a desk or sitting on easy chairs around a coffee table with them? When a fellow manager asks for something, are you responding in the most friendly, helpful way you could? After a while, these things should become automatic, but to begin with managers will need to stop and think.

Honing Your Deadly Skills: **You will also need to teach managers the seven deadly skills of communication in this book. They are all skills which every manager can and should practise, and they can all be applied in any organization whatever its size, industry or anything else.**

Making the change

Your managers will need a huge amount of support from you if this is going to work. It's no good just saying 'This is what we want you to do', handing them a copy of this book (although that will help) and leaving them to it. They will need training, support and feedback from you for a long time, so be prepared. Brief senior and middle managers before you announce the changes to everyone else, answer their questions and tell them what training you'll be giving them.

If the survey shows that you are popular with your staff but there is a little room for improvement, you may be able to shift attitudes quite easily. But if you have a significant way to go, the only way to do it is to make a splash. You can't just run a couple of management training and briefing sessions and then sit back and watch.

Burn your bridges

The first thing to do is to commit yourselves totally by telling all your employees what you are doing and why, admitting your failings and telling them what you intend to achieve and how. Make it a big thing. Burn your bridges. Do it on a significant date such as the beginning of the year, the launch of a new product or simply the first of the month. And you must start the moment you announce it. You can't say 'We've decided you deserve to work for a more supportive organization, so we'll go on treating you badly for the next two and a half weeks, but from the 1st July we'll change.' Tell them 'As of today, 1st July, things have changed round here.' Now you'll make the most enormous fools of yourselves if you don't follow through, quite apart from damaging morale beyond repair.

Offer something concrete

People are suspicious, especially if your track record as an employer isn't good. They'll think you're all talk unless you give them a taste of what to expect immediately. So tell them that as from now every manager, from the board of directors down, will be focusing on the three key words the staff themselves chose in the survey. Managers aren't going to change personality, but they are going to exercise a different attitude. Give them some examples – memos will now say 'please' and 'thank you' on them, pay packets will now be prepared early for people who are going to be working out of the building on the last day of the month – come up with some initiatives you can announce at once. And try to find at least one big initiative which reflects the key focus words. Announce that you are introducing flexitime, or that you are going to train everyone who wants it towards vocational qualifications, or some other company-wide scheme.

One thing which helps to convince people that things really have changed is to institute regular team or departmental meetings which are attended by someone higher up the organization than ever before – a senior manager or director. They don't have to make it to every meeting, but they should be there more often than not and when they can't make it they should send a deputy. Where communication is poor, people get very frustrated and feel that none of their comments ever get through to senior management. But this way, they can tell them what they think face-to-face; this gives people the feeling that their voices are at least being heard.

Support your managers

You will need to train your managers well – you're asking a lot of them. This doesn't have to mean paying for lots of expensive courses. If you want everyone to pull together, you need to train them in-house, at least primarily. You may well need to call experts in for a few training courses initially, but you should soon reach the point where you can run your own training, or hold sessions for managers to discuss problems and challenges between themselves, and help each other to find solutions.

Your managers don't just need a few training courses; they need constant support. Senior managers will need to give support and real help and co-operation to the subordinate managers, and be available when they ask. Don't launch an initiative like this just before a big conference or event which is going to occupy top management; they will need to be around a great deal for the first few days, and readily available to hand-hold for several weeks.

Keep the initiative going

The very hardest part of all is keeping the momentum up. The danger is that after a few weeks things will start to drift back and after a few weeks people will look back on the whole event as yet another management failure. This is why all the managers' initiatives should be long-term ones. You should also schedule in regular – and frequent – reviews, ongoing management training sessions, and so on.

You also need to make sure that you don't make any promises you can't fulfil *to your employees' level of expectation.* If you make a grand speech announcing that you are introducing flexitime, think how your staff will feel when it turns out that only 10 per cent of them are eligible for it. If you offer training for all, imagine how demoralized they will be when they find that their managers can't actually schedule in the time for them to attend training. Far better to promise less and deliver on your promises, than to promise more and fail.

Be prepared to wait for results

Changing your image with your employees takes time. It will certainly take months; it can take years. The longer the negative image persisted, the longer it will take to replace it with a positive image. The staff will start by thinking that it's just another one of those management navel-contemplating exercises. After a while, they'll think 'This is good . . . but it won't last. Never does.' But gradually, if you keep the momentum going, they'll start to be convinced. And new staff will arrive who don't know how it used to be and are less sceptical. If you stick with it, it will work. Promise.

Your mission statement

A good mission statement gives everyone in the organization a collective purpose; it helps to unite everyone and it gives them a touchstone against which to measure everything they do. If it doesn't help to fulfil the mission, it isn't a priority. If it contradicts the mission statement, they shouldn't be doing it at all.

If your organization has no mission statement, or has one which is badly devised or ineffective, it is time you produced and used a well-considered one. If you are overhauling your corporate personality along the lines just set out, this is the ideal time to overhaul your mission statement as well. The mission statement is central to what you do and should therefore be considered and agreed by the directors and senior management. It's not just something the marketing manager or personnel director cooks up and circulates without reference to the board.

In fact, the process of creating the mission statement can be as important as the statement itself. The more managers are involved the better, because it will help them to focus on what the organization is really all about. This exercise is important in itself, whatever choice of words you finally come up with.

What should it say?

The mission statement is there to state why the organization exists. It isn't about your goals, or how you will achieve your aim. It simply confirms your *raison d'être*. It should be succinct enough to be memorable, and concrete enough to be understood. Don't write guff such as: 'to offer high quality outdoor residences created to maximize their beneficial aesthetic qualities in order to facilitate maximum satisfaction.'

There are four main guidelines to follow when you write your mission statement:

➤ focus outside the organization, on your customers and potential customers;

➤ be altruistic in your approach;

➤ disregard any results which follow on from achieving your mission (such as profits, more jobs and so on);

➤ simply ask yourself: what are we here to do?

For example, if your organization makes luxury summerhouses and gazebos, your mission might be: *to provide well built, beautiful garden buildings which people will enjoy using.* It's as simple as that. One brief, clear sentence which describes what you're there for.

What do you do with it?

Mission statements have a bit of a reputation in some quarters for being a waste of time. That's because they are all too often used badly

– which generally takes the form of not being used at all. But research indicates that a well-used mission statement helps customer service programmes to meet their aims. And good communication, although it starts internally, is also intended to improve external customer relations.

Making the most of your mission statement means:

➤ Make sure that everyone in the organization understands the mission statement and how their own job contributes to fulfilling it. If you ask any of your employees what the organization is there for, they should all give you the same answer.

➤ Put a copy of the mission statement on every department's notice-board.

➤ Put a copy anywhere visited by customers – reception areas and so on – and send every customer a copy of it.

➤ Maintain enthusiasm for the mission encapsulated in the statement by talking about it and showing everyone by example how to believe in it and work towards it. Use it in company training and briefing sessions so that no one loses sight of it.

Summary

Identify your corporate personality

Your organization has a corporate personality as far as your employees are concerned, whether you like it or not. You need to identify this corporate personality, by surveying your staff, to see whether it should be improved:

➤ make sure the survey is anonymous;

➤ survey everyone;

➤ give them a reason to respond to the survey;

➤ tell them what you will do as a result of their responses;

➤ analyse the results collectively, or in large groups;

➤ ask people to identify the characteristics they associate with the organization and those they would like it to possess.

Change your corporate personality

➤ identify the personality you would prefer, from your employees' response to this question on the survey;

➤ change the organization by changing the attitudes of the people in it;

➤ change must come down from the top – the very top;

➤ ask each manager to come up with three initiatives to back up the key word focus for change;

➤ train each manager to think about all their significant interactions with others in the light of the key focus.

Making the changes

➤ burn your bridges by announcing big changes;

➤ offer something concrete to show you mean business;

➤ support your managers with help and training;

➤ keep the momentum going after the initial burst;

➤ don't expect miracles – lasting change will take time.

Your mission statement

➤ a mission statement describes what you are there for;

➤ it should be brief, clear and focused outside the organization;

➤ it is worthless unless it is used.

2 *Written Communication*

There are times when you should communicate with your staff in writing, and times when it is better to speak to them directly. This chapter is all about written communication (Chapter 3 will look at verbal communication). The first thing to establish is when to communicate in writing. The six key methods for written communication are:

➤ memos;

➤ notice-boards;

➤ letters to staff;

➤ e-mail;

➤ faxes;

➤ internal newsletters.

Once you have established that you need to communicate in writing, and which method to use, the next stage is to learn to use the techniques of written communication effectively. So this chapter will also establish how to say what you intend to, in a clear and straightforward way.

When should you communicate in writing?

If you have something to communicate to one or more of your staff, there are generally only two ways of doing it: you can write it down, or you can say it. And it can make quite a lot of difference which you do.

Honing Your Deadly Skills: **Written communications give a very different impression from verbal ones – think how you feel when you receive a letter compared to the way you feel about a phone call. Saying something in writing lends it weight; it's more formal, and it seems more authoritative. This can be a good thing, but it isn't always appropriate.**

Advantages of writing

Here's a run down of the pros and cons of communicating in writing. Written communication is a good idea when . . .

➤ You want to impart an air of formality and authority.

➤ You want a permanent record of exactly what you have said.

➤ There are legal reasons for putting down what you want to say in writing.

➤ You are communicating with a number of people and you want everyone to receive exactly the same information.

➤ You are communicating something complicated, which people will take in better if they have it in writing.

➤ You have something very important to say which must be seen to be formally communicated. However, you should never spring big surprises on people, such as company shake-ups, in writing – announce them face-to-face and follow them up with written confirmation.

➤ It is quicker (a fax can be faster than a phone call, for example).

➤ You want to avoid the lengthy discussion which can follow from a face-to-face communication of information – but don't write in order to get out of a necessary discussion; if employees need to ask questions you should be available. However, if you need to confirm something which has already been discussed in depth, a written communication can save dredging up the whole debate again to no purpose.

➤ You need to be diplomatic and may not express yourself as well as you would like verbally. By writing, you can choose your words carefully.

➢ You want everyone to know that a particular piece of information is on the record. For example, you might congratulate an employee on exceptional work in the company newsletter – that way they, and everyone else, know that the recognition is public.

➢ You want someone to have a record of your thanks or congratulations to keep.

Disadvantages of writing

Don't choose written communication when:

➢ The people you are communicating with need to ask questions or seek clarification.

➢ More discussion is needed before facts are established.

➢ You want to promote a friendly, informal atmosphere (unless there is an overriding reason why you need to put the communication in writing).

➢ The information you have to impart is very important (although you can confirm it in writing).

➢ The information you need to communicate is highly confidential and any leaked documents could be seriously damaging.

➢ The information may be upsetting to the recipient.

Choosing your method

Having established that the information you want to communicate would be best put across in writing, you still have to choose your approach. Should you jot it down in a memo, or send a letter to each of the staff? Or would it be better to impart the information in the company newsletter? Sometimes it's obvious which method to use, but often it isn't. Different methods of communication do give a very different impression, and it can matter which you use.

Memos

A memo somehow seems less formal than a letter when it is circulated to a number of staff. It doesn't give the impression that what it has to say is weighty (although it might be important). This gives you the opportunity to strike a relatively informal note while still putting down information which needs to be in writing. For example, you might want to circulate the dates of forthcoming meetings or events. A memo will seem friendly and informal, but the dates are down in black and white.

Here are some additional points to bear in mind if you are considering circulating a memo:

➤ Memos are often read and then thrown away, after any important information (such as dates) has been transferred. So don't use a memo to communicate information which you want people to retain.

➤ Memos are generally regarded as a fairly public form of communication (they are not traditionally distributed in a sealed envelope), so you should never use a memo to transmit confidential information.

➤ While a memo which is circulated to several people seems informal, a memo directed at only one person comes across as a formal version of a conversation. Are you sure a conversation, or an e-mail, wouldn't be better?

➤ Memos shouldn't be used to impart bad news. For one thing, a letter or e-mail would be more confidential. And for another thing, the informality of it becomes distasteful: if the news is bad, the least you can do is make the effort to send a proper letter, although bad news should normally be given face-to-face. But even if the news is only moderately disappointing, a memo can still come across as flippant and uncaring.

Notice-boards

Be very wary of using company notice-boards. There is very little which is appropriate to them. The biggest problem with them is that a lot of people don't read them, or read them so rarely that some notices pass them by entirely. This means that you can only use a company notice-board to impart information which might never reach its target. Not much can happily fall into this category.

Notice-boards are much better run by staff for themselves, with someone sensible in charge to make sure that nothing unsuitable is pinned up. The board can then carry teams and dates for the company football team, notices about sponsored cycle rides and photographs of the PR manager's new baby. If you want your employees to feel like part of a big family, especially one which has little or no inter-departmental rivalry, a notice-board can be a very good thing. But it is not a suitable vehicle for managers to transmit operational instructions to their colleagues or employees.

Letters to staff

A letter is a private form of communication between two people: that is what it is useful for. There is really very little point in circulating a letter to several people. If the information is very important you shouldn't be giving it in writing at all. If it isn't private, you'd be better off sending a memo round. The only exception is where the general information is public, but the details aren't: for example, everyone with a company car is getting a letter about their new vehicle, but they have been allocated different cars and this information is being imparted privately.

Letters are mostly suitable when you are communicating with only one of your staff. If you have something confidential to say, a letter is more formal and personal than a memo, and shows that you have given thought to the matter. You might be responding to a request for a budget increase, or replying to a complaint against the organization, or passing on a copy of their appraisal sheet. Or you might be giving a disciplinary written warning.

Sometimes the information should be given verbally, but backed up with a letter. If you turn down a request for more staff, or extra budget, this may well be better explained in person. But giving the person a letter to confirm the decision shows that you have treated the request seriously and gives them a written record which they can keep.

E-mail

E-mails are much like letters, in that they are a private, one-to-one communication. But they do differ in some important respects:

➢ They are generally seen as being less formal than a letter.

➢ They are much less likely to be printed out and kept permanently.

➢ Since they are very personal, you can use them effectively to make a public communication seem personal. For example, some MDs regularly e-mail all their staff to let them know what they're up to. This only works if the content of the e-mail is personal, at least to the sender. You can't effectively e-mail everyone with important news of how the business is doing – this should be done through team briefings (which we'll look at in Chapter 5). But if MDs tells everyone about their latest business trip, how fascinating it was to see the Japanese approach to business first hand and invite any comments back by e-mail, it makes them appear more approachable to the staff.

Faxes

A fax has the personal touch, with the informal air of an e-mail. However, it is different from an e-mail because:

➢ A fax is not confidential.

➢ It is a permanent record, unlike an e-mail (which can be printed out, but often isn't).

Faxes are most useful for putting businesslike information into writing, to confirm or clarify facts or arrangements, or for circulating press cuttings. They are not a medium for imparting brand new information, or for giving disappointing news.

Internal newsletters

Internal newsletters are an important instrument of communication and one that is rarely used as well as it should be. But they are a great way of imparting all those small but necessary pieces of news, such as keeping people posted on the plans for refurbishing the reception area and for recognizing successful employees. They are also a terrific medium for trumpeting good news.

However, a newsletter is not the way to impart important company news, which should be transmitted in person. Nor is it the place to announce bad news, such as poor profits. You can refer to them, but they should already have been announced. A newsletter should have an upbeat tone; anything which doesn't fit this doesn't belong in the newsletter.

Most importantly, don't use the newsletter as a medium for the MD or CEO to write long tedious articles about 'how well we're all doing but times are tough and we must all keep the pressure up . . . blah, blah, blah'. People just won't read it. Would you? It is a great mistake to focus on what the management wants to say rather than on what the employees will be interested to know. What's more, it will create and perpetuate a 'them and us' relationship because employees will feel (quite rightly) that they are being talked down to.

The biggest general mistake people make with internal newsletters is not to take them seriously enough. They don't think them through properly and then they delegate them to someone else – often without a clear briefing – and ask them to sort it out when they have time. Of course they never do have time and before long the monthly newsletter comes out every four to five months, if you're lucky. This is terribly demoralizing to staff who feel that they personally have been put at the bottom of the priority list.

Producing a newsletter
Here are a few dos and don'ts to make sure your newsletter is well produced and serves a useful purpose:

Do

➢ Decide before you start exactly what you're trying to achieve. For example, the newsletter could be designed to:

(a) improve staff morale;
(b) enable management to inform staff of company news;
(c) enable people and departments to talk to each other;
(d) create a feeling of unity among departments or subsidiaries which are spread out.

Once you have set your objective, use it to determine:

(a) what kind of topics you will cover;
(b) what the tone of the newsletter will be (serious, light-hearted, full of jokes and crosswords, or whatever).

➤ Recognize that your staff will judge your attitude to them by the way you handle 'their' newsletter. If you put a lot of effort into getting it right, you will give the impression that they are important to you. If, on the other hand, it's put together in a hurry and keeps being shoved to the bottom of the priority list, this tells your staff that they're not very important to you. Getting each issue out on time should be top priority.

➤ Find somebody reliable and good with people to run the newsletter, and make it a prestigious job and part of their job description. It can be a difficult task in a lot of ways, particularly trying to persuade people from other departments – perhaps even more senior people – to write articles to a deadline, so give your editor all the support you can. Alternatively, you could employ a company which specializes in producing internal newsletters – but you will still need a liaison person inside the organization to help generate articles.

➤ Treat the newsletter as an important management function and set a good example. Make it clear that if someone agrees to write a piece for you, you expect them to do it by the deadline. Never allow people to say 'I'm really pushed – still, this is only an article for the newsletter, so it can wait.'

Don't

➤ Don't use the newsletter to disseminate important news to your staff. This is absolutely the worst, most impersonal and demoralizing way to hear important news from management. However, you can certainly communicate minor pieces of news or supplementary information through the newsletter. For example, don't use it to tell employees that you're moving offices, but do use it to give them regular updates afterwards on how the new building work is going, or how many people visited the exhibitions stand at the NEC.

➤ Don't abandon the newsletter once it is set up – it signals to your staff that they're not important. If you're not sure you have the resources to produce an issue every month, start off more modestly – say, once a quarter – and build up if and when you feel able. Equally, don't get carried away in terms of size or design either: start small and get bigger, not the other way round.

Writing effectively

You've established that you need to communicate in writing and now you have decided which method will be the best. But you still have to write whatever it is you want to say. A lot of managers, quite understandably, hate this bit. In fact in surveys, many managers cite writing as their least favourite part of the job. You know what you're trying to say, but you can't seem to get it to come out right on paper.

 Honing Your Deadly Skills: **Writing effectively is really very easy to do, but you have to know the guidelines and, unfortunately, very few managers are trained in the essential skills of business writing.**

One of the best ways to learn about business writing is to think about the letters, memos, faxes and e-mails you receive. What makes them useful? Which ones are hardest to follow? Most frustrating or demoralizing to read? Whose letters and memos do you dread, and why? Make a point of noting your reaction to the written communications you receive for the next couple of weeks and try to analyse what causes your reaction.

There are two aspects of any written document to consider: structure and style. In what order will you present the facts and which words will you use?

Structure

It's easy to spend ages trying to decide which order to say things in and what exactly needs saying. Some of the communications you receive need reading two or three times before they make sense, so you know it's important to get it right. But there's actually a very simple formula to follow which helps you structure any piece of writing from a memo to a newsletter article. The mnemonic for the formula is SCRAP:

➢ Situation

➢ Complication

➢ Resolution

➤ Action

➤ Politeness

This gives you a structure to write to and it also makes it much easier to see what should be included and what information is a waste of time. Crucially, the SCRAP formula helps you to keep your writing brief, without leaving out anything essential. You know yourself how unpopular long letters and memos are, and this system will help you avoid being one of the guilty ones.

You will find that this formula works for everything, although if you are simply confirming information, or giving an instruction, in writing you won't need to use the first two steps (situation and complication).

Situation

The first thing to do is to state the current position, so that the recipient of the communication knows what it is about and understands the starting point for what you have to say. For example, if you're e-mailing a colleague to ask when they are available so you can set up a meeting, the situation is: *We need to meet with Lisa and Bob to discuss the NEC exhibition.* It's as simple as that – you're just stating what you're writing about.

Sometimes you need to explain the situation – perhaps the e-mail is going to someone who doesn't know about the exhibition yet – but you can still be brief: *We're going to be running a big, prestige stand at the NEC exhibition next April, for which we're building a completely new stand.* A letter would not be the place to start explaining the details. You can send them a copy of the original report, or the minutes of the meeting where the show attendance was decided, or ask them to call you if they want the details – but don't bore them with it on the screen. At the moment, you're simply explaining the reason for the e-mail – the situation – you haven't yet reached the main point, which is about setting up a meeting.

Complication

The next step is to explain what is complicating the situation so that you have to write. If there were no complication, there would be no letter, e-mail, fax or whatever. In the example of the meeting about the exhibition, the complication is that everyone has a very busy schedule and Bob is away for the whole of the second half of June.

If this weren't the case, you'd simply send an instruction to say that the meeting is on Friday at 11.00. So the complication is: *Everyone has a very busy schedule and Bob is away for the whole of the second half of June.* That's all you need to say.

Resolution

If you have a complication, you need a resolution to it. So what are you proposing to do about it? Once again, you can be brief – you simply need to explain how you're going to get round the problem: *I am therefore suggesting that everyone gives me a list of available times between now and June 14 when they can spare up to two hours. I will fix a meeting date as quickly as possible and e-mail you back.*

Action

It's a good discipline to include this step every time to make sure that you remember to stipulate what you want the other person to do, so that you are both absolutely clear about who should do what, and by when: *Please e-mail me by the end of tomorrow (Thursday) so that I can get back to you with a confirmed date before the end of the week.*

Politeness

The written word is always prone to appear more brusque than face-to-face conversation, so make sure you finish every communication on a polite note. This can be simply a matter of saying 'Many thanks', or 'Best wishes', but it is a lot friendlier than simply signing your name. You might choose to say something more, such as *I thoroughly enjoyed our lunch last week; we must do it again soon.*

A flexible formula

And there you have it. A simple, five-stage formula for writing clear, concise business letters, faxes, memos and the rest. The only thing we've covered which it doesn't always work for is newsletter articles: we'll look at how to structure those in a moment. Here are two more examples of the SCRAP formula in action:

A personal letter turning down a request to attend a conference

Dear Sam

(*Situation*) You asked me a few days ago if you could attend the conference on 'New Developments in Packaging' in Edinburgh at the end of next month. The visual aspects of packaging are important to your job so I have given your request a good deal of thought.

(*Complication*) The problem is, however, that the conference clashes – as you know – with the final trial run of the BW 194.

(*Resolution*) I simply don't feel I can spare you for three days at such a crucial time, so I'm going to have to say no to the conference.

(*Action*) Please let me know if any other similar conferences crop up in the future, as I would be happy to let you attend if the timing is less problematic.

(*Politeness*) Thank you for showing interest in attending the conference, and I'm sorry I can't give you a more positive response this time.

Best wishes,
Jackie

A memo asking everyone to tighten security

To: All staff
From: Paul Robbins, Personnel Director

(*Situation*) In the past, we have always left the doors leading off from the reception area open so that everyone can come and go between departments freely.

(*Complication*) Unfortunately, in the past month, two handbags and a watch have apparently been stolen from offices near to the reception area. As you know, reception is very busy at times and our receptionists cannot always keep as watchful an eye as they would like.

(*Resolution*) The only effective solution is to keep the doors permanently closed and to use the security keypads every time. As an extra measure, we will be changing the security codes in the next few days. (*Action*) So please would you make sure that in future you remember to keep the doors closed.

(*Politeness*) Thanks for your help.

Paul

Writing newsletter articles

Newsletter articles don't generally follow the SCRAP formula, unless you're simply imparting information. But don't worry; there's a simple formula for articles, too. If you always follow exactly the same formula it can become rather repetitive, especially if the newsletter is a long one with a lot of articles in it. But this formula always works when you can't find an effective alternative. (It is also, not surprisingly, the way to write press releases.) A newsletter article should state:

➢ what;

➢ who, where, when, why and how;

➢ any other details.

What

If you're a natural raconteur – or if you've ever listened to one – you'll know that the way to tell an anecdote is to save the punch line until the end. Well, the way to write a good article is just the opposite: you have to start with the punch line. When you pick up a newspaper, what do you do? You look at the headline and, if it catches your interest, you read the first paragraph to see what the piece is about. If the first paragraph doesn't tell you what the thing is about, more often than not you'll give up and read a different article.

People are fairly impatient when they read news articles, and you have to respond to this by giving them the crux of the piece straight away. For example: 'A key member of the dispatch department has just been given a substantial cash bonus as a thank you for making a suggestion which has cut our costs considerably.'

Who, where, when and why

Now people want to know the rest of the story; you've given them an outline – now fill in the details. Make sure you remember to answer all five questions: who, where, when, why and how, in whatever order seems to make most sense:

> B(*Who*)Michael Chan, our Mailing Supervisor, was given a cheque for £500 by Personnel Director Jo Billings, (*Where and when*) at a special departmental lunch last month. (*Why*) Michael realized that with a simple redesign on the standard plastic boxes we pack our products into, we could reduce the overall weight of each package we send out. This would bring the packages down in weight to a lower charge band, saving us nine pence on every standard package. (*How*) The present packaging boxes include a tuck-in flap which runs the length of the box. Michael suggested this be replaced with a small tab which fits into a slot in the front of the box. After talking to our suppliers, they are now producing the new design at the same price.

Any other details

You've got the whole story down now and anything else you say is optional. You don't need to say any more in order to explain the story to your reader; the rest is purely for interest. A good newsletter article should generally be no longer than about 250 words (the example here is up to about 150 so far). A feature article might be a little longer, but research shows that shorter articles are more likely to be read than longer ones in company newsletters.

You may not have a lot of space to say more, or you may not feel there's anything interesting to add. That's fine – no one minds reading short articles. But if there is anything else which might interest readers, say it at this point, after the key pieces of information. In particular, use quotes from the people in the story to give the article a more human dimension. For example:

> Jo Billings pointed out, 'We send out an average of over 150 packages a day, so Michael's suggestion saves us around £70 a week. We're absolutely delighted that he came up with such a simple but ingenious idea.' The thought first came to Michael when he weighed one of the packages and noticed how close it was to the lower charge band. 'I wondered how to reduce the weight,' he explained, 'I started cutting pieces off a few of the

boxes and experimenting before I came up with the idea of adapting the tuck-in flap.'

Style

Even once you know what order to say things in, it is still possible to become tongue-tied – or keyboard-tied – over the words you use. We all have a tendency to worry about how we come across in writing, despite the fact that few of us worry about how we're about to come across when we're speaking – we just get on with it. And that's the technique for writing: just get on with it, as if you were speaking. The closer your written communications are to polite speech (avoiding slang or extreme colloquiallisms), the better written they will be and the better you will come across. You are aiming for a natural style.

There are certain styles to avoid when you write, which you will no doubt recognize (from other people, of course, not from yourself).

The bureaucratic haze

Some people love to fill their writing with big words and convoluted sentences. They seem to think it will impress people and make them appear more important than they are (the people who are *really* important almost never do this). So they will say, for example:

> It has been brought to the attention of the undersigned that, notwithstanding directions to the contrary, certain employees have been availing themselves of vehicular parking facilities which have been allocated to the sole use of visitors. It is requested that all recipients of this communication terminate this practice with immediate effect.

What they mean – and what they should say – is: 'Apparently some people have been parking in the visitors' spaces in the car park. Please don't.'

The sea of waffle

Another popular fault is to go into lengthy and unnecessary detail in writing about things which, if they need to be said at all, should be said face-to-face. For example:

> There are 53 car parking spaces in the car park, and four motor-bike spaces, which should be ample room for everyone to park.

However some people seem to be using the visitors' spaces, of which there are three since, after lengthy debate, it was decided last year by the customer services department that there are almost never more than three visitors at any one time. These spaces are the nearest to the front entrance since it was felt strongly that customers should not have the inconvenience, especially in bad weather, of having to walk further than necessary

. . . and so on.

Fighting talk

Just as we are prone to road rage when we are sheltering behind the anonymity of the car, so people tend to feel more confident about hurling insults and insinuations from the safety of the printed page. Far too many managers make inflammatory remarks in writing which they wouldn't dream of expressing so strongly face-to-face. Rudeness is always starker in black and white, and this kind of communication is deeply demoralizing and unpleasant when directed at junior employees. When aimed at colleagues, it creates or inflames rivalry between managers and departments, which is never in the interest of the organization. For example:

Some people seem to be under the impression that ordinary parking spaces aren't good enough for them, and have taken it upon themselves to rise to the status of visitors. Would these people perhaps like to wear an identifying badge so we can all doff our caps to them when we pass them in the corridor?

Would you want to work for someone who talks to you like that? So long as you avoid these unnecessary styles of writing, there are only a few simple rules to follow to make sure that everything you write is clear, readable and polite, which is really all you need to achieve.

Keep it short

The shorter your communication, the more pleased the recipients will be. When have you ever picked up an eight-page letter and thought 'Ooh, goody!' You need to be as brief as you can without leaving out anything important. We've already seen how the SCRAP formula gives you a quick reminder of everything that needs to be covered, and can help you avoid being too wordy.

Keep it simple
But keeping it short doesn't only apply to the memo, letter or whatever it is as a whole. In order to keep your writing simple and easy to read you should also use:

➢ short, simple words;

➢ short, simple sentences;

➢ short paragraphs.

Long words don't impress, they simply make things harder to read. Some long words are unavoidable of course – there isn't a shorter alternative to polystyrene, for example – but choose a shorter word if you can. Don't say 'requirement' if 'need' will do; and why say 'facsimile' when you could just say 'fax'?

Some words may not be long, but are unfamiliar or difficult; avoid these too. For example, the word 'milieu' is actually shorter than 'locality', but it is not so easy to take in. People find it much easier to read words they are used to. By the same token, long and convoluted sentences don't make people think you're clever (pompous, possibly, but not clever), but they will confuse your readers.

The visual layout of the page is important, too. A page with plenty of paragraph spacings and insets looks much more approachable than one which is a solid wodge of text. So start a fresh paragraph for each new thought and leave a clear line between paragraphs.

If you find it harder to express yourself in writing than face-to-face, you're not alone. But there's a simple trick to use when you find yourself chewing the end of your pencil, or playing aimlessly with your mouse, trying to find the right words. Imagine the person, or people, you are writing to is standing in front of you. Start talking out loud and say whatever it is you want to communicate. You should find that you have no trouble finding the words when you are speaking; then simply write down what you have just said. You might need to tweak it a little bit, to remove any slang or adjust any phrases which seem ambiguous once they are written down, but it should come out pretty well as you want it. Remember, you're not trying to win the Nobel prize for literature, you're simply trying to transmit information politely, clearly and readably.

Beware of appearing rude
When we speak, we employ a great deal of body language, which we are mostly unaware of. It only really becomes evident when it is missing: when we write. You can say things face-to-face which come across as being friendly and positive because your facial expressions, your stance and your gestures show your meaning as much as the words do. But put the same words on paper, without the body language to back them up, and they can seem sharp, rude and even aggressive.

Read this sentence: 'In future, make sure the agenda is circulated at least a week in advance.' This can come across as an order, and a slightly irritated one at that. But if you read it out loud, you'll see that it might well have been meant as a polite request. Sentences like this have a tendency to come across as being sharp or brusque when you often didn't intend it. You could easily soften the example above by saying 'In future, please could you make sure the agenda is circulated at least a week in advance.'

You'll remember that the SCRAP formula stipulates some kind of politeness at the end. A letter, or even a memo, which ends without so much as a 'Thanks' or a 'Regards' tends to seem rude or offhand. So read your communication through before you send it off, and look out for phrases or sentences which unintentionally come across as being sharp or abrupt.

Beware of being ambiguous
The danger of ambiguity when you write extends beyond the possibility of appearing rude when you didn't intend it. People often read sentences with a different emphasis from the one you would have used if you had been speaking it aloud. Suppose you write to a junior employee: 'I'm disappointed that you can't make the meeting.' This could be interpreted as meaning anything from 'It's a bit of a shame you can't make it' right through to 'You've let me down badly by not being there', according to the interpretation the reader puts on it.

This doesn't necessarily mean you shouldn't say it, but you need to be aware of what it could mean to the reader. Perhaps they're the type of person who will always put the best interpretation on things. Or perhaps the tone of the surrounding letter or e-mail makes your meaning clear. Just make sure you read through the communication keeping an eye out for this kind of ambiguity.

The most frequent culprits in cases of ambiguity are words like 'fairly' and 'quite' and 'a little'. When we speak, we use them to mean anything from 'very' to 'slightly'. When we write, the reader doesn't have a clue which of these extremes we intend. For example, try saying 'It's a fairly important point' out loud a few times using a different emphasis each time. You can make it mean anything from a moderately important point to a very important one. In writing, the reader will interpret it one way and probably never even realize that it might have meant something different.

Another word to keep a look out for is 'worried'. This is used to mean anything from mild concern to deep anxiety. If your boss writes to you 'I'm worried about your last month's sales figures' should you simply explain the figures more clearly, or should you start drafting your resignation? Again, if you try it aloud it can mean almost anything.

Summary

Written communication gives a different impression from verbal communication, so the first thing you should do when you have something to impart is to decide which of the two you should use. Compared with speaking, written communication is:

➢   more formal;

➢   more permanent;

➢   better if you want to be sure you choose the right words;

➢   less confidential.

Having decided to communicate in writing you need to choose the best method. These may include:

➢   Memo
  • less formal than a letter;
  • more likely to be read and then binned;
  • not confidential.

➤ Notice-board

- may never be read;
- most suitable if you run it by staff, for staff.

➤ Letter

- private;
- personal;
- lends weight to its subject.

➤ E-mail

- private;
- less formal than a letter;
- less likely to be kept than a letter.

➤ Fax

- personal;
- public.

➤ Newsletter

- public;
- not suitable for bad news;
- most useful for minor but necessary news items.

You have selected your medium, and the next stage is to say what you want to as briefly and effectively as possible. There are two aspects to this: structure and style.

Structure

For memos, letters, e-mails and faxes, follow the SCRAP formula:

➤ situation;

➤ complication;

➤ resolution;

➤ action;

➤ politeness.

For newsletter articles, follow the order:

➢ what;

➢ who, where, when, why and how;

➢ any other details.

Style

Avoid styles which are bureaucratic, waffly or inflammatory and:

➢ keep it short;

➢ keep it simple;

➢ beware of appearing rude;

➢ beware of being ambiguous.

3

The Third Deadly Skill

Verbal Communication

Most people find face-to-face communication far easier than expressing themselves in writing. But the fact that it's easier doesn't necessarily mean that it's more effective. In fact, the reverse can happen: it's so easy we don't stop to think about it, which means that we don't necessarily say what we mean to in the way we intend. We upset people with an unfortunate turn of phrase, or confuse them with an ill-thought-out 'explanation'.

This chapter will look at the various ways of communicating with people verbally:

➤ telephone;

➤ one-to-one meetings;

➤ departmental or inter-departmental meetings;

➤ presentations;

➤ company meetings.

Having looked at the options, we will then examine the techniques for effective verbal communication:

➤ choice of words;

➤ tone;

➤ body language.

Finally we will look at the crucial skill without which verbal communication cannot be effective:

➤ listening.

When should you communicate verbally?

As we saw in the last chapter, there's a good deal of difference between written and spoken communication, in terms of the effect it has. Your choice of medium says a lot about your intentions. In general, spoken communications are more informal than written ones and they invite more of a response: the other person is on the spot to question you, ask for clarification or even disagree with you.

So you should think carefully about which approach you use and consider the impression you give. If you consciously choose the best approach you will find that it doubles the effectiveness of the communication. Suppose you want to let one of your employees know that you are turning down their request for three extra days of holiday after they have used up this year's entitlement. If you tell them to their face, they will take this approach as an invitation to argue and keep trying to persuade you. If, on the other hand, you write them a pleasant but firm letter, the formality of the approach and the fact that your decision is written down, gives a clear signal that the matter is now closed.

Here's another example. Your department has collectively let you know that they can't stand the drab conditions any longer and they want to redecorate the offices, even if they have to do it themselves. Instead of circulating a memo to let them know you are considering it, you call them together for a meeting about it. Before the meeting even starts, you have sent a signal which says you are open to reasonable suggestions and you want to hear what they have to say. Even if you end up deciding you can't redecorate, you've made them feel you cared about their views and wanted to help.

Advantages of verbal communication

It's worth having a look at the main reasons for and against verbal communication, starting with the plus points. Verbal communication is a good idea when:

➢ you want to appear informal;

➢ you want to invite suggestions and ideas which are more likely to be sparked off in discussion;

➤ you are explaining something complex and people might need to ask for clarification as you go along;

➤ you have important news to impart, such as company moves and shake-ups, or bad news for the team or organization;

➤ you need to be very diplomatic and feel you will be more effective face-to-face than in writing; this is often the case because you can watch their response and adapt to it as you proceed;

➤ you have personal bad news to impart (such as news of being turned down for promotion, for example);

➤ you have something highly confidential to say and can't risk it being put down in writing.

Disadvantages of verbal communication

There are times when verbal communication really isn't appropriate. Of course there will be times when information falls into this category and also into the 'avoid written communication' category; you'll just have to decide which wins on balance. Maybe the information is too confidential to write down, but for legal reasons you need a permanent written record – you just have to weigh the facts and choose the lesser of two evils.

More frequently, you will find some information can be imparted either way – through a phone call or informally in writing, perhaps via fax or e-mail. In this case, you are free to choose whichever you find quickest or easiest.

However, let's just summarize the kinds of information you should avoid giving verbally. Don't choose verbal communication when:

➤ you want to maintain formality or distance from the other person or people;

➤ you want a permanent record of what has been said (unless you produce this as a follow-up document or minutes);

➤ you need your comments to be in writing for legal reasons;

➤ you want to avoid further discussion of the subject by signalling that the matter is closed.

Choosing your method

As with written communication, once you've decided to speak rather than write, you still need to select the best approach. There are various options and each has its own strengths and weaknesses. Should you pick up the phone, or call the person into your office? Do you call an ordinary meeting, or would a presentation be better? Sometimes there is more than one good option, but often one approach is more effective than any other.

I'm not suggesting that you should never pick up the phone to make a quick call without first thinking through the options of calling a meeting or giving a presentation instead. Just be aware that there can sometimes be alternatives – and better ones, at that. It can be helpful to stop and think before every communication for a set period of, say, a week. This exercise should make you more conscious of the options generally and when you should choose each one.

We all have types of communication we make regularly in our jobs and after a week you will have covered most of them. At the end of the week, you may find that your weekly round of phone calls to junior managers asking for the week's figures has turned into e-mails, and that you have decided to incorporate a presentation into your regular management meeting every time there's a new project to propose. Once the trial week is over, you still need to stop and think before each new or irregular kind of communication, but you won't need to do it every time.

Telephone

A phone call is easy, informal and private, and generally requires no forward planning. If you want to hold a meeting, even a one-to-one meeting, you need to get your diaries out and fix a time. But a phone call is immediate, even though you might need to leave a message for someone to call you back if they aren't available. There are several points worth bearing in mind about phone calls:

➢   If you aren't sure of the reaction your communication will receive, a phone call can be better than a letter or e-mail. For important news, you need to talk to someone face-to-face, but less important news can still generate unexpected reactions. The phone gives you a chance to gauge the response you are getting and adapt your words or your tone to it. For example, suppose someone submits a report which needs more work done on it before you can use it. When you break the news, the person might be defensive, upset, panicky about the workload, or depressed that the report didn't come up to scratch. Over the phone, you can conduct the conversation to suit their response. In a written communication, you're committed before they ever read it.

➤ The phone also gives you a level of privacy you can't achieve face-to-face. This makes it much easier to mask your feelings. If you are worried that you're going to lose your cool with someone, perhaps another manager who is frequently obstructive, it can be better to talk on the phone than face-to-face. That way, you can maintain a better relationship with them by concealing your anger, or only showing what you feel is appropriate.

➤ Since it is possible to conceal feelings over the phone which you don't want to reveal, it's no surprise that you can also inadvertently conceal feelings which you *do* intend to show. As with written communications, the lack of body language signals will hamper your communications if you don't substitute verbal signals for visual ones. For example, you can't show you're listening by making eye contact and looking interested, so you have to make 'Mmm-hmm' noises more often, and repeat back key phrases to show you've taken them in.

➤ There is no permanent record of a telephone call. If you ask someone over the phone to do a certain thing, you cannot later prove that you ever asked them. If you are communicating with someone who can be absent-minded or even underhand, a written approach may be better.

➤ If you are imparting a simple piece of information, such as the date of a meeting, a fax or e-mail will often be quicker since you won't get caught up in conversation. But a phone call can be quicker than a face-to-face meeting. For one thing, people just accept that a business phone call is generally a quick, functional thing. And for another, it is far easier to get off the phone than to get someone out of your office who doesn't want to leave.

Telephone skills

You must have noticed that some people are easier to talk to on the phone than others. Some chat on for hours, or are short to the point of rudeness. Some simply leave you with the feeling that they haven't really taken in what you were saying. So here are a few guidelines to make sure you're one of the ones with a reputation for being easy and productive to communicate with by phone:

➢ When you make a call, start by saying who you are. It can be very disconcerting for the other person to have to guess. A simple 'Hello Jo, Mike here' is much friendlier than just launching into your spiel leaving the other person to catch up.

➢ Likewise, when you answer a call, say 'Hello, Mike Lawrence' rather than simply 'Hello' or 'Yes?' I know the caller ought to know whose number they dialled, but they can still be caught off guard if you answer very promptly, or when they had almost given up, or after your voice-mail has cut in. Saying your name gives them a moment to collect their thoughts, as well as sounding friendlier.

➢ You can hear a smile down the phone. Sorry to sound like a platitudinous new ager, but it's true. If you want to seem friendly, smile, especially when you say hello. If you don't smile, you can come across as sounding false if you are saying something which would call for a smile in a face-to-face dialogue.

➢ If you call someone up and expect the call to take more than a minute or two, always start by asking 'Have you got five minutes?' (or ten, or however long you think you need).

➢ If you have more than two or three points to make, write a note of them and tick them off as you go.

➢ If you are too busy to take calls, don't answer them when they ring – have them diverted or switch on your voice-mail. However, if you do answer them for some reason – perhaps there's one call you're waiting for – stop the person before they start, don't let them get half-way through what they're saying before you rudely cut them off. Be ready before you pick up the receiver to deter the call if you need to: 'Hello, Mike Lawrence'. 'Hello Mike, Jo here'. 'Hello, Jo. Actually, I'm in the middle of a meeting. Can I call you back after lunch?' Needless to say, you should make a point of calling back when you say you will.

➤ Show you're listening, as we saw earlier, by making 'uh-huh' and 'mmm' noises, and repeating back important points: 'So you need it by Friday at the latest . . . '.

➤ Concentrate on the call. You know *you* can tell when the person on the other end of the phone is actually opening their post, signalling to someone else or using their computer when they're supposed to be talking to you. Well it works both ways. Don't kid yourself *you* can get away with it – no one can. Not only is it very rude, you may miss an important part of the conversation without realizing it.

➤ Don't give orders over the phone; make requests. So instead of saying 'Hang on', say 'Could you hold on for a moment?'

Before you make a call, be prepared for the person you are calling to be out. Are you going to leave a message, and if so, what? You can always leave your name and the time and ask them to call you back, or tell them you'll try again. The question is, will you say any more than that? If you don't decide in advance, you often end up leaving waffly messages

It's about the meeting next week. Or rather, it might not be next week . . . well, that's what I'm calling about really. I don't know whether you're free on Tuesday afternoon, or are you going to be at the Liverpool office – I need to talk to you about it really. Um . . . maybe you'd better call me back this afternoon. Oh, before four, because I'm out after that . . .

. . . and so on. It hardly gives a good impression. What is worse is when the subject of the call is slightly sensitive and you can't decide on the spot whether to explain to the secretary what it's about, or whether to be elusive. So always decide in advance what you'll do if you need to leave a message.

Conference calls

I said earlier that the telephone is a private, one-to-one method of communication, but of course there's an exception to that: the conference call. You can link up as many people as you want to and hold a meeting over the phone. Or you can hold a central meeting with a speakerphone on the table to link to anyone who can't be there in person.

The first thing to say about conference calls is that unless the number of people involved is very small they are far from ideal. Often they are the best option and they are enormously valuable when people are too far apart to meet up face-to-face, but with more than three or perhaps four people involved they will always be a flawed method of communication. It's important to be aware of the drawbacks:

➤ Face-to-face, people use body language to gauge whose turn it is to speak and when. If several people are vying to speak, the order they speak in is often decided by the group by common consent and signalled because everyone looks at that person. Over the phone, you can't even hear who else is trying to speak, let alone choose whose turn it is. You need a very firm and clear-headed person in the chair. Even so, there is a danger that the discussion will go too far the other way, and people will stay silent too much of the time because intervention seems pointless and ineffective: this can have a dampening effect on people's tendency to spark new ideas or original approaches to problem-solving.

➤ It seems a very basic point, but you can't always hear people properly down a phone link, especially with a speakerphone on the meeting table. The people on the phone are at a distinct disadvantage to those in the room and can find it difficult to make their point heard at all.

➤ In a face-to-face meeting, everyone has to pay attention pretty much. But in a conference call, people can be talking to someone else in the room with them, or finishing something off on the computer and it won't be noticed. The more people in the call, the more each one can get away with. You can sometimes even get away with leaving the room for a couple of minutes and no one will know you've gone.

If you do have to use conference calls – and there are times when you do – they are much better for meetings without conflict and without a need to generate lots of ideas. They are at their best when they are used for planning and scheduling meetings, for example, or for project updates.

One-to-one meetings

This kind of meeting covers appraisal, counselling and discipline interviews, but also covers other meetings such as meetings to impart bad news – or good news – and progress meetings with individual employees or colleagues.

One-to-one meetings are the face-to-face version of a phone call: a private, verbal communication between two people. But they are very different in terms of the impression they give.

➢ Phone calls *are* private, but they often don't need to be. The privacy is usually incidental, and not the reason for choosing to use the phone. One-to-one meetings, on the other hand, are almost always chosen *because* they are private, especially meetings with employees (rather than fellow managers). Generally, a one-to-one meeting is chosen because the matter to be discussed is confidential.

➢ One-to-one meetings are also useful for discussions or briefing on work which would take too long to talk about on the phone, or which require both parties to look at drawings, drafts, samples or something of the kind which would be physically impossible over the phone. However, this kind of one-to-one meeting is less common for the simple reason that these meetings generally call for more than two people to be present.

➢ Although verbal communication is less formal than writing to someone, a one-to-one meeting is more formal than a telephone call. The fact that you make an appointment to see each other raises the status of the meeting to something more considered and important than a quick phone call.

➢ It is unusual to take minutes at a one-to-one meeting, since you are both focused on each other it would be intrusive to do more than take a few notes. However, one-to-one meetings are frequently followed up with a letter confirming what has been said or agreed. So this kind of meeting can be preferable to a phone call if you want a written record of what has been said.

The techniques of one-to-one meetings are covered in Chapter 6.

Departmental or inter-departmental meetings

This kind of meeting is by far the most effective way for a group of people to communicate directly. E-mail can work if you are exchanging information or making the occasional comment, but group meetings are the way to handle interactive discussion, debate or information exchange between three or more people.

A badly-run meeting is a waste of time, as most people know all too well from experience. Chapter 5 covers the key points of how to run an effective meeting. But assuming the meeting is well run, it is the medium to choose every time for making decisions which require the input of several people. It is also the best way to brainstorm problems or generate new ideas, since people spark off each other and the whole becomes greater than the sum of its parts.

There are three functions which a meeting can fulfil: it can inform, discuss or decide. Most meetings combine at least two, if not all three, of these functions:

1   *Inform.* A meeting is not the place to give out factual information which could have been circulated as a memo or report. But sometimes a meeting is needed if the information needs clarifying or if people might want to ask questions about it. A verbal progress report on a project the group is responsible for keeps people feeling more involved than a memo would.

    And some things are too important to be passed on in writing: if you are reorganizing the department and people's jobs and responsibilities will change, informing them face to face shows that you recognize the importance to them of the changes. A plain memo would be insulting and dismissive.

    If you're reorganizing the department and most of the staff don't know yet, you may not want to put anything down on paper until it has been decided. Some things are best discussed in meetings because they are too sensitive to put in writing.

2   *Discuss.* Meetings are the place to bounce ideas around, argue over new policies, debate proposed targets for the group and so on. This kind of discussion can't be done any other way and the interaction of the group will spark ideas or solutions that would never have been thought of otherwise. These kinds of meetings must include everyone who is relevant to the project, policy,

target, or whatever is under discussion. Excluding people from the meeting will make them feel excluded from the result of the meeting. Why should they work to a target they never helped to set?

3   *Decide.* Most meetings, apart from those intended purely to inform, end up as a time-consuming form of navel-contemplation unless they end up making decisions. The decision may only be to collect certain information or establish certain facts before the next meeting – but if nothing happens as a result of the meeting, what was the point of it? The minutes of a meeting should record who will carry out each action and by when.

Making decisions and agreeing actions is the point of most meetings. You can achieve the same result as a manager simply by sitting alone in your office and then issuing instructions to your team, but often a meeting is the better approach. You can hear other people's input, you can secure their agreement and the process means that each person can see how their role fits in with the rest of the group – for example, if they don't design the survey by the end of October, the sales people won't be able to circulate it at the exhibition in the second week of November.

Meetings are also useful from a social point of view:

➤ They give a group a feeling of identity and unity, and make people feel they are one of the team.

➤ They also help people to recognize the contribution which they make individually to the group and what difference it makes to everyone else.

➤ A meeting is also the fairest way to make everyone feel they have had a democratic say in decisions, even if their view didn't win through. This helps to generate a feeling of commitment to decisions which the meeting makes.

Presentations

If you have something to say to a group of people, either to inform them or persuade them to a certain decision, a presentation can be the way to do it. A presentation is different from most other forms of verbal communication in that it is, essentially, one-sided. You may take questions during it, or people may raise points afterwards, but it is accepted that if you are giving the presentation you get to choose if, and when, you can be interrupted.

A presentation is a very useful tool if you have anything to say which calls for advance preparation and which is better said without interruption. (We'll look at the techniques for doing this in Chapter 4.) This doesn't mean you can give a presentation any time you fancy saying something without anyone arguing back. But if you want to explain to senior management how you are planning to increase revenue over the next 12 months if they give you two more staff, offer them a presentation to explain it clearly.

Equally, if you want someone on your team to explain a new system, or give a progress report, to the rest of the team you might ask them to give a short presentation. This might be incorporated into a meeting, or it might be given separately. It can be particularly useful if you have people on your team who are prone to interrupt and argue, and you want this information put across clearly and without interventions.

Company meetings

There are times when it is necessary to call the whole organization, or large parts of it, together and talk to your employees all at once. The reasons for doing this are:

➤ The news you have is very important, such as a reorganization, redundancies, a new working system, or something else which will affect everyone's working life.

➤ You want everyone to hear the news simultaneously, so people's sensitivities won't be hurt by being the last to hear the news.

This is the only way to impart big news to people. If you can't get absolutely everyone together, at least be seen to have done your best and make sure the people who aren't there are told directly as soon as possible by their manager. Telling people face-to-face shows you care about them and recognize the importance to them of what you have to say. If the news is positive, this technique really helps to generate organizational loyalty. (It is often a good idea to try the speech out on senior managers first; they can point out bits that may confuse or upset or antagonize their own staff.)

You can't take questions at this kind of meeting or you'd be there for ever. But people need to ask questions. So brief managers fully and then make sure each one holds a section or departmental meeting within the next 24 to 48 hours to answer any questions. If there is a danger of employees being upset, angry or resentful, the longer the wait before the meeting, the more upset, angry or resentful they will become. Try to hold this kind of meeting early in the week, otherwise feelings will become entrenched over the weekend.

Speaking effectively

What you say is important, of course: it's why you picked up the phone or called the meeting. But it's not the whole story. If you don't express yourself clearly, and in the right manner, you will not achieve the effect you want. You may not put your point across clearly if you choose the wrong words; you may upset or discourage people if you employ the wrong tone and you may confuse people if you don't use appropriate body language.

Choice of words

As with written communication, you need to keep your words as short and simple as possible. This is much easier to do when you're speaking, since a natural speaking style tends to be simpler, but you still need to be conscious of it. You should be especially aware of your choice of words when you are speaking at more formal occasions such as presentations or company meetings; it is much easier on these more formal occasions to slip into the kind of pompous style that employs long words where short ones will do.

If you have something to say which is likely to confuse, upset or anger the person you are going to say it to, don't risk waiting until you get there to see which words come out of your mouth. Think about the clearest way to explain something, or the kindest way to put what you have to say.

Just because you're speaking and not writing, it doesn't mean that everything has to be impromptu. Even if you don't choose the exact words for fear of sounding rehearsed, you can still consider the best order to say things in. If you were explaining a bicycle to someone who hadn't a clue what it was, would you start by explaining what it looked like, or what it did? If you're telling someone they've been turned down for promotion, do you start by giving them the bad news straight out and then telling them why, or should you explain the background first to soften the blow? It will help to think through things in advance and then let the words come naturally to fill in the structure you have prepared for them.

Tone

It's tempting to talk about manner rather than tone – in a sense that is what I mean – but manner is something you evolve and acquire over years and you can't just change it on demand. It's no good telling someone who has a gruff, blunt manner which they have had for 40 years that they must be soft and gentle. However, a gruff person is capable of adopting a softer tone – it may not be as soft as the next person's, but that doesn't matter. The person they are talking to will judge them by comparison with their usual style, not by comparison with someone altogether different.

What matters is that you adopt a tone which is appropriate to the occasion. Watch other people, and note how their tone does or doesn't suit the purpose. You can learn a great deal. People respond to tone on a subconscious level and are generally completely unaware of it consciously. But the wrong tone can stimulate a reaction which you don't want. For example:

➢ An irritated tone will deter people from asking questions about something which they don't understand and should be encouraged to ask questions about.

➢ A brusque tone will upset someone to whom you are breaking bad news and magnify the strength of their reaction.

➢ A relaxed tone will encourage people to keep talking in meetings when you actually want them to be brief because time is short.

➢ A curt tone will make a word of thanks sound less sincere than an expansive tone.

➢ A friendly tone will make a criticism sound less serious (which may be what you want, or it may not).

Your tone of voice will send out a signal which can be as strong as the message your words are giving. If it contradicts the words, as in the examples above, it obviously dilutes or even cancels out what you are saying in the minds of the listeners.

If you're wondering why your words don't have the effect you want, the answer often lies in your tone. If your meetings always overrun despite your entreaties to the participants to hurry up, listen to yourself next time, and see if you really sound as hurried and anxious to get on with it as you want *them* to be. If the people you call into your office to give disappointing news to always seem to get more upset or defensive or angry than you think they should, perhaps your tone is encouraging this response. If you come across as tough or aggressive, people often get upset or defensive. If your tone is tentative, they may take advantage. So think about what tone to adopt before any potentially tricky encounter, and suit your tone to the occasion.

Body language

As with tone of voice, our body language gives signals which should reinforce the words we are saying. If these signals contradict our words the listener will be confused, without understanding why, and will find our words less convincing. If your body language is natural, relaxed and confident:

➢ your posture will be relaxed, and perhaps leaning forwards just a little towards the other person when they speak to show you are listening;

➢ your arms will be by your sides or loosely in your lap (assuming you're not writing or carrying things);

➢ you will make regular eye contact without staring;

➢ your gestures will be open (without being wildly animated).

If your mood is not relaxed and confident, your body language is likely to show it. If you are uncomfortable or nervous:

➤ you will fidget or shift position more;

➤ you will avoid eye contact or only make occasional eye contact;

➤ your posture will be hunched or held in, with legs or arms crossed – or both;

➤ your gestures will be minimal and will tend to be closed – for example, rather than raising your arms you might prefer gestures which involve moving your hands only.

By contrast, if you are being aggressive or domineering:

➤ you will lean forwards;

➤ you will hold almost constant eye contact;

➤ your gestures will be over-expansive;

➤ your legs and feet will be planted apart;

➤ you will use gestures which involve finger-wagging, fist-clenching or other aggressive moves.

You can't consciously control your body language every second; you wouldn't be able to concentrate on what you were saying. But you can run a quick check on it every so often – at the start of the conversation, any time you notice your emotions taking hold (nerves, anger or anything else) and any time you notice the person you are speaking to adopting marked body language in response to you. If they recoil, for example, or move towards you aggressively, note what signals you're giving off.

Listening

 Honing Your Deadly Skills: **This book is not about the seven deadly skills of issuing edicts, or delivering monologues. It is about the seven deadly skills of communication and you can't communicate alone. Someone else has to be involved and they have to be able to respond. If the communication is verbal, they will respond verbally – and you will have to listen in order to complete the process.**

Listening is not only about hearing, it is about taking in what the other person has said, and letting them see that you have absorbed it. You don't have to agree with it, but you must give it a fair hearing. Do you remember as a child telling your mother or father excitedly about some new discovery, only to receive the response 'Really, darling? How nice' and knowing that they weren't really listening at all?

It is incredibly frustrating when someone doesn't really listen to you properly, and even though they answer when you speak, you know they haven't really taken in what you said. So the skill of listening is not only about hearing, but also about showing that you have heard. There are certain techniques you can use when people are speaking to make them feel that you are listening:

➢ show that your attention is on them;

➢ make eye contact;

➢ be relaxed but lean forwards slightly to show you are attentive;

➢ make listening noises, such as 'mmm' and 'uh-huh';

➢ repeat key points back to them (without breaking their flow): 'So it's just like a photocopier really, but it puts the information into the computer instead of on to paper? I see.'

The most important thing you can do when it comes to listening is to do it properly. There's no point in trying to fake all these techniques (although if you did, you'd probably find you had listened after all). The best way to convince someone you're listening is to do it. Whether you're on the phone, in a one-to-one meeting or at a meeting with several people, if you are genuinely concentrating and focused on what the speaker is saying, it should come across.

Summary

Verbal communication gives a very different impression from written communication and you should choose it for different occasions. Compared with writing, verbal communication is:

➤ more informal;

➤ less permanent;

➤ better if the news you have to impart may be upsetting to the recipient;

➤ better if you want to give the other person or people a chance to question or comment.

Having decided to communicate verbally, you need to choose the best method. These may include:

➤ Telephone

- immediate;
- informal;
- private.

➤ One-to-one meeting

- confidential;
- more formal than a phone call.

➤ Departmental or inter-departmental meeting

- allows for group interaction;
- to inform (with the chance to ask questions), discuss or decide.

➤ Presentation

- persuasive;
- one-sided (you control interruptions).

➤ Company meeting

- for very important news;
- everyone hears the news at the same time.

You have chosen your medium, and now you need to put your message across as effectively as possible. This involves making the right choice of words and tone, and being aware of your body language.

Choice of words

➢ always use simple language, even when speaking to large groups;

➢ think through the best way to say something in advance.

Tone

➢ adopt a tone which suits the occasion;

➢ if people don't respond to what you are saying, consider whether your tone is sending out a conflicting message.

Body language

➢ your body language should give the same impression as your words and tone;

➢ aim for a relaxed posture, with regular eye contact and open gestures, to appear easy and confident;

➢ make a mental check on your body language every so often, especially if you don't feel as relaxed as you'd like to appear.

Listening

Finally, but crucially, communication is a two-way process, and you cannot do it properly unless you learn to listen:

➢ concentrate on the speaker;

➢ show that you're listening.

4

The Fourth Deadly Skill

Communicating with Senior Management

Unless you are at the very top of the organization, you will have managers or directors senior to you with whom you need to communicate. For a manager, this is one of the most important elements in achieving a successful and motivated department, as well as being one of the keys to personal success. Many managers really start to rise in the organization when they get noticed for a particularly professional and persuasive presentation or report.

This chapter is about the most important routes to making yourself heard at senior management or board level, and how to get your point across most effectively. The key techniques for this are:

➢ identifying the best lines of communication upwards;

➢ making your point at meetings;

➢ giving internal presentations;

➢ writing reports.

 Honing Your Deadly Skills: **Once you have mastered these skills, you will find that you become a highly effective link between your team and top management; a link which will enable both you and your team to work more effectively and more rewardingly.**

Identifying the best lines of communication

You know what your official line of communication is up through your boss to their boss and so on up to the top. In a relatively small organization, you may well be only a step or two away from the top. In a huge organization, you can have thousands of people working for you and still be three or four steps away from the people right at the top.

It makes a big difference if your route to the top is an effective one: if your boss always argues convincingly on your behalf to their boss, who in turn puts your case well to the next person. This kind of system gives you support when you need it, wins you the resources you need, and means that a smooth path is cleared for you and your department to get on with the job you are there to do. Resources, extra staff, a revised date for a big event, training you feel you or your team need, a change of system when you complain that the current one doesn't work – all these things can be manifested when your upward line of communication is clear and effective.

But what if the line isn't clear? Suppose your boss is very un-organized and constantly frazzled and never gets around to helping you acquire the resources you need. Or perhaps they just don't get on with their boss, who never looks favourably on any proposals which come through them. Or perhaps your communications go astray or grind to a halt further up the line. Few managers are lucky enough to have a perfect line of communication to the top, and some have a very weak communication route indeed. And of course, the more layers of management there are, the greater the chance that there will be a weak point in the line.

So what can you do, other than be defeatist and give up altogether? Well, there are several things you can do, and you'll need to decide – perhaps through trial and error – which works best for you. But before you can try anything, you need to identify the problem.

Identify the problem

You can't remedy the weak point in the line until you know which point it is. So you must start by finding out which manager or director is obstructing you. Often, you know the answer to this; in many cases it's obvious. But if you're not sure, start with your boss. When you ask them to pass a proposal or a request up the line, check with them whether they have. If they always say that they have decided not to, or that they will but they haven't got round to it yet, clearly the problem lies with them. If, however, they always tell you that they have but they haven't had a response back yet, you can ask them to help you identify the weak point. Again, unless there are numerous layers of management, your boss should know where the problem lies. If not, they can talk to their boss and so on up the line; identifying the weak point is generally not too difficult.

The next stage is to establish the nature of the obstruction. Are your communications being blocked deliberately or through inefficiency? Is there someone in the communication line who doesn't want your proposals to get through, because they favour another department, or have a grudge against your boss, or privately don't believe that your department should have such a high profile? Or is your culprit just inefficient and never gets round to putting forward your proposals and requests, which are well down on their own priority list?

 Honing Your Deadly Skills: **Know your enemy: before you can begin to resolve the problem you must know where the weak point is and why they are blocking your communications. And bear in mind that the longer the line, the more possibility there is that there may be more than one weak point. Don't assume when you have cleared the first blockage that there isn't another one further upstream.**

Deal with the problem

If the communication system is blocked there are two ways of dealing with it: either clear the blockage or sidestep it. Which solution you choose will depend on the nature of the problem. But whichever solution you choose, there is one thing which will always help: put everything in writing. We'll look at how to write reports later in this chapter, but even if it doesn't warrant a full report, at least your communication can go into a letter or memo. Don't use e-mail or, if you do, back it up with a memo or letter, because you want to be sure that everyone in the line of communication has a copy on paper. That way everyone, right up the line

➢ has exactly the same communication;

➢ can be furnished with a replacement copy if they lose their original copy;

➢ knows that the communication originates from you.

Clearing the blockage

If the obstruction in the line of communication is the result of inefficiency or accident, you can generally find a way to encourage the person concerned to co-operate with you more. You'll need to find a technique which suits the nature of the problem. If the person concerned is:

➢ *Unorganized* and always delays your communications while they clear their permanent backlog of paperwork, you need to get your communication to the top of their in-tray. You may be able to enlist the help of their secretary or assistant (who will be even more aware than you of their boss's shortcomings). Or you can keep reminding them – unorganized people are so used to this that they don't usually mind; they just assume that everyone's life is full of phone calls which start 'Have you remembered . . . ?' Sometimes you don't feel you can do this however, and you can't always persuade your boss or someone else between you and the culprit in the communication line to help. In this case, disguise the call. Phone about two or three days before they should be presenting the document and say, for example: 'I assume you'll be presenting my proposal at the half-yearly budget meeting on Wednesday, so I thought I should give you a call to ask if you have any questions, or need any supporting papers to go with it?'

➢ *Absent-minded* and forgets or loses your communications, put everything in writing and then keep reminding them. If you don't feel you can nag your superiors, get someone else to do it – your boss, or the person's secretary. But with most people it's not a problem to call once a week or so to check whether they have dealt with the matter yet. If you expect them to put forward your proposal or request at a particular meeting, call them a day or so before it to remind them.

➢ *Frequently away* from the office you will need to work on your timing when you submit any proposal or request. Ask their secretary or assistant to tell you when they are going to be around so you can make sure that you, or your boss, arranges for any paperwork to land on their desk at the best time.

Sometimes a deliberately obstructive person can be persuaded to unblock the system; it's often worth a try. The best way to handle it is head on, but without being confrontational. Arrange to have a few minutes in private with the person concerned. Ask to see them, or arrange a lunchtime drink – whatever suits your relationship. Then say something along the lines of: 'I wanted a word because I get the feeling that you're not happy about the proposal I put forward, and I'd be grateful if you could explain what's bothering you?'

If the root of the problem is not a personal grudge but a specific reluctance over this particular issue, and especially if this isn't a regular problem, you may well find this helps. Often the answer is simple. Maybe they just don't care for the proposal, in which case you might be able to persuade them round to your point of view, or at least persuade them that the board should have the opportunity to discuss the matter. Maybe they will convince you that your proposal is flawed, in which case perhaps you can rework it so you are both happy.

There is absolutely no point in confrontation because the other person will simply become more entrenched. Either you will resolve the matter amicably or you won't resolve it at all. So if you don't think you (or they) can keep it friendly, it would be better not to use this approach.

Overcome the obstruction
There are times when none of the techniques above work – when you simply can't clear the blockage. In this case, you will have to find an alternative route to the top. Either you can hop over the person concerned and go straight to their boss, or you can find another route entirely. The trick is to find a way of doing this without appearing to snub the person in question – who is, after all, one of your own bosses.

Getting past the obstruction   If you have put your communication in writing, simply make sure you (or your boss) distribute it to the culprit's boss – the next point in the communication line – as well as to them. You might distribute it to several other people as well, if it is relevant to them. So if the obstructive manager does nothing about it you won't mind, because other people will take action. You can also step over the obstruction without causing obvious offence by issuing the communication when they are away on holiday or at a conference or exhibition. If you can create some kind of urgency ('we needed an answer before we could commit ourselves to next month's production schedule') you have a perfect excuse for not waiting for their return.

Stepping over the obstruction is all about finding excuses for going to their boss, rather than antagonizing them by showing them up or deliberately snubbing them. You will have to accept that if they were deliberately blocking your communication they won't be happy if it gets through whatever the means, but at least you don't have a confrontation to deal with – and your communication has made it through. If the person concerned is very difficult you may need to pick the communications you really care about, rather than employ this technique too frequently.

Sidestepping the obstruction The other way of overcoming the problem is to take a different route to the top altogether. The way to do this is to find someone else, who is effective and helpful, through whom you can communicate with top management. Suppose you are the production manager, and you have a proposal for a new system which will improve the quality of your products but will cost more, at least in the short term. Your production director is not putting your proposal to the board because their immediate concern is to keep costs down. You feel strongly that the board should at least discuss this proposal, despite the short-term costs, but your director won't budge.

The way to sidestep the blockage is to go to the quality director with your proposal. After all, it's a quality issue, so it's a perfectly reasonable thing for you to do. You can often sidestep like this, by taking communications relating to budgets through the finance management line, communications about anything to do with customers through the marketing channels, and so on.

If you don't want to rile the manager in question, there are ways to get round the problem. If you involve another manager after your line manager has blocked you, it can look manipulative. But you can distribute your proposal or request to the other manager at the same time as them; you'll have a pretty good idea when you're going to meet a blockage so you simply take action before it happens.

Another way to avoid riling the obstructor is to switch communication channels several steps down the line from them. Suppose the problem person is two levels of management above you. You could put your proposal to a manager in a different communication line who is only one level above you – or even to a fellow manager at your own level – so by the time it reaches the level of seniority of the obstructive boss it is already heading off up a different line altogether.

Do as you would be done by

One last point on the subject of clear lines of communication: make sure you aren't guilty of blocking communications from the people who work for you. Make sure you set an example so that your team is motivated and its members feel that their voice can be heard, and also so that senior management can see what they should be doing. It is easier sometimes to pursue a point on behalf of your employees than on your own behalf. If your bosses witness you working on behalf of your team members, they are more likely to follow suit themselves.

Making your point at meetings

There are few things more frustrating at work than being unable to get your point across and the problem is at its most immediate in meetings. You can go into a meeting with strong views about something on the agenda and an hour later you emerge without having had the chance to say what you wanted. There are only two people you can blame for this: yourself or the person in the chair. Either you have failed to express yourself effectively, or they have failed to give you the opportunity. But either way – even with a weak chairperson – you can get your point across if you know how.

The key is preparation. You have to know in advance what you want to say, and you do that by going through the agenda items and considering each point. Some may not be particularly important. Some may not concern you personally to any great extent. Some you know will bring general agreement anyway. What you're looking for are the points which you feel strongly about and which may take some work to persuade others to agree with you over.

Less is more

The less you say, the more people will listen when you do speak, especially if what you say has a reputation for being worth listening to. Think about media sound bites – the media broadcast these because they know that we are more likely to take in the key point if it is stated once clearly, than if we hear it wrapped up in arguments and explanations and justifications.

The more people dominate a meeting and do all the talking, the less notice others take of them, and the less often the chairperson invites them to comment. You need to decide in advance on your sound bites – the few essential points you want to make – and aim to say as little as possible the rest of the time. That way it is bound to be your turn to speak by the time you actually want to.

Not only should you decide what you want to say, but also how you want to say it. Just as if you were writing a presentation (a skill we'll look at in a moment), you should find the clearest way of saying something and the way with the most impact. I don't mean script it word for word and then recite it, but find a convincing analogy, or a perfectly chosen example, to make your point succinctly. And when you have made it, don't elaborate if you can help it. If people ask questions, answer them without going off on a ramble, and reiterate your main point rather than confusing people with numerous minor arguments.

There are also some useful techniques for deterring people from interrupting you in midstream:

➤ Make eye contact with everyone you can.

➤ Take your time – don't gabble.

➤ If people are itching to butt in, pause for breath in the middle of a sentence (when it would be rude to interrupt) rather than at the end (when they can pretend they thought you'd finished).

➤ If you have, say, three key points to make (which should be your maximum), say 'I have three points to make . . . '. Again, it's much harder for people to interrupt before you reach the end.

Lay the groundwork

There is one other way to help get your point across at meetings and that is to recruit the chairperson to your cause. After all, they control who gets to speak at the meeting. If you feel you have a particularly important point, or a valuable idea, let them know in advance. Depending on your relationship with them you can either have a word with them, or send them a note outlining your point, asking them to ensure you have an opportunity to make it during the meeting. A good chairperson wants to encourage valid and useful contributions, and they will usually be very happy, when the agenda item comes up, to say 'I know Jack has an interesting idea about how we might be able to solve this . . . '.

Giving presentations

Every manager has to give presentations from time to time and an audience of your own senior management or directors is possibly the most nerve-racking of all. Many managers would rather give a presentation to 40 or 50 customers than to four or five top managers in their own organization. Not only is the subject of your presentation going to be assessed by them, but so are you. You know that their judgement of your performance may well influence future decisions about your career in the organization. No wonder most managers feel nervous.

The remedy to this fear is simple, of course: just make sure you give such a polished and effective presentation that any impact it has on your standing in the organization is bound to be positive.

Honing Your Deadly Skills: **All the techniques of good presenting are very straightforward to learn. And the secret, once you have learnt them, is simply to prepare and rehearse thoroughly until you are so confident of what you are doing that there is no room for nerves.**

So what are these techniques for giving confident presentations? The process has six component parts:

1   planning;

2   research;

3   structuring;

4   writing;

5   visual aids;

6   delivery.

Planning

Once you know that you have a presentation to give, the very first thing to do is think. Work out what your objective is: what you want your presentation to achieve. Let's suppose that you are giving a presentation to the board of directors about your recent trial direct mail campaign. What you want to achieve is to convince them that it is worth investing in a nation-wide campaign.

An objective should always be written down; it gives you a focus and functions as a touchstone against which you can assess every piece of information you research to see whether it should be included. If it helps towards the objective, it should go in. If not, it shouldn't. So obviously, to be useful, you need a fairly specific objective. Simply aiming 'to talk about the recent direct mail trial' is not going to be very helpful. A written objective should state three things:

➤   the subject of the presentation;

➤   who is in the audience;

➤   what they will gain from the presentation.

In this case, your objective might be: *To give the board of directors a summary of the recent direct mail campaign and its results, to demonstrate why it is worth investing in a nation-wide direct mail campaign.*

The other aspect of your presentation you need to plan at this stage is the schedule. It's very easy to leave a presentation until the last minute, especially if part of you doesn't want to think about it because it worries you. But if you do this, you make all your problems worse and you hugely increase the likelihood of persuading the board of directors that your performance is a bit shoddy and you don't seem to have prepared it very professionally. Even if the facts speak for themselves and you get the go ahead for the nation-wide campaign, you may still miss out on the next promotion that's going.

The schedule doesn't have to be complicated for an internal presentation to a group of senior managers. You're not doing a huge product launch with a stage and fancy lighting and press packs and a big audience and products which might not be ready on time. So the schedule isn't complicated; but it must be done. The simplest way to do it is to look at the next four stages in the process – research, structuring, writing and visual aids – and for each one, set the following:

➤ diary sessions blocked in to fix the time when you plan to do the work;

➤ the final date by which you will have this stage of the process complete (and mark this date in your diary).

The completion date for each stage will ensure that if you don't do the work when you scheduled it in your diary, at least you will know as you go along how far behind you are slipping. However, it really shouldn't come to this. Internal presentations are extremely important to the good of your department and for your own career, and only the most extreme emergencies should justify getting behind schedule at all.

Research

Now you have your objective, you should be able to work out the main points you need to make. Clearly, in the example above, you need to focus on the key points about the trial campaign, and then on what this tells you about future costs and future return on that investment.

Having worked out these main points, the next step is to assemble all the information you could possibly need in order to make them. Collect together the figures on the trial campaign – costs, staff time, results, percentage response, type of orders placed and so on. And assemble all the figures for your proposed nation-wide campaign. Talk to other managers who would be involved and get information from them: the dispatch manager will tell you what is involved in getting the mailshot out, the production manager can tell you whether it will be possible to meet the orders if the response is high. Talk to your marketing consultants about the best way to handle the campaign, to the printers about producing the mailshot material, to the Royal Mail about postage costs, and so on.

Look at each piece of information in the light of your objective: *To give the board of directors a summary of the recent direct mail campaign and its results, to demonstrate why it is worth investing in a nation-wide direct mail campaign.* If the information contributes to meeting this objective, keep it. If not, discard it.

The next step is to write out each individual piece of information on a separate piece of paper. This is not as laborious as it might sound and it will save you a lot of effort later. You only have to jot down a note of the key point and if there is a lot of supporting information you can write a reminder on the back of the paper telling you where to find it. If you use a word processor, you can simply type in a list of notes, print them out and then cut the paper up so each point has its own slip of paper.

When all the information is transferred to these slips of paper, organize them into related groups. Perhaps all the information about the costs of the trial campaign will go into the same group and all the information about the expected response to a national campaign will go together. When you come to structure your presentation, which is the next stage, you will put these groups into an order, but the pieces of information within each group will almost always stick together.

Structuring

Virtually all presentations are intended to sell something and this is as true of internal presentations as of presentations to customers. You may not be selling a product, but you are selling an idea. In our example, you are selling the idea of investing in a national direct mail campaign. Your presentation is designed to persuade and you should never lose sight of this; it is the basis for the structure of the whole thing.

There is a useful formula, known as the four Ps, which you can employ to structure any presentation:

➤ position;

➤ problem;

➤ possibilities;

➤ proposal.

Position

The first thing to do when you begin your presentation is to state the present situation. For example, you might want to say that you have always promoted your products in the past through advertising and teleselling.

This summary of the current position doesn't have to take long – anything from about 30 seconds to three or four minutes – but it is important. When you give a presentation you are acting as a guide, leading your audience through the jungle of information, pointing out the interesting features along the way, and making sure that they all arrive together at the right place on the far side. The first thing any good guide does is to assemble the party at the beginning of the journey, making sure everyone is ready. Clarifying the current position means that everyone is starting from the same place, and they all know it.

Problem

The next thing to do is to establish the problem – in other words, the reason why something has to be done. Why can't we just go on advertising our products? Again, this needs clarifying so that everyone else understands exactly why the group has to navigate through this jungle at all. So for the benefit of anyone who can't see the need for change, or is open to it but doesn't understand the reasons for it, you need to state the problem – for example that advertising and teleselling are becoming less and less cost effective. If it is uncontroversial and generally accepted, this may only take a sentence or two, but it needs doing.

Both the 'position' and the 'problem' sections of your presentation form an introduction; it is essential, but it may not be lengthy. The remainder of the presentation contains the real meat of it.

Possibilities

This section does not appear in every presentation (sometimes it is excluded and you have only three Ps). This is where you outline the options; the alternative routes you could take through the jungle. In some presentations there is no choice of options; in this case you move straight on to the final stage – the proposal.

But often there is a choice of routes and you need to explain what they are. If you are presenting the results of a trial, or research or survey findings, these will obviously determine the possible courses you could follow, so they need to be explained at the beginning of this section of your presentation. The key to doing this is to keep it as brief as you can. Don't spend hours wading through detailed statistics – that isn't what a presentation is for. Only present the key results. You can always circulate the full findings either in advance of the presentation or after it, for anyone who needs them. Their function at this point is simply to support and explain your arguments – they are only a means, not an end in themselves.

Now explain what the possibilities are. For example, you could run a national door-to-door leafleting drive, or you could run an advertising campaign backed up by direct mailshots, or you could run a direct-mail campaign alone.

You should present an unbiased view of these options; people can't be expected to form opinions or draw conclusions until they have all the facts, so don't impose judgements at this stage. By the time you complete this part of the proposal, everyone should understand exactly what the relevant information is and what possibilities it gives rise to. But as yet, you haven't given any indication of which possibility you recommend.

Proposal

Now is the time to explain which of the possibilities you recommend, and why. Be careful not to pooh-pooh any of the options, because some of your audience may have favoured that route and to condemn the idea is a criticism of their judgement. So give the impression that they are all valid but explain, using the data you have collected to support your case, why the option you are proposing is the best.

You might say, for example, that the trial results indicate that a direct-mail campaign will be far more successful than advertising and needs to be run alone to assess its precise results; it can later be combined with advertising and the comparison will then be available to judge the most effective method after that.

Not all presentations offer a range of possibilities, in which case this stage of the proposal follows straight on from outlining the 'problem'. If you had already decided, as a company, that you were going to run a direct-mail campaign nationally if the trial was successful, your aim would be simply to demonstrate that it had succeeded. In this case there would not be a range of possibilities, but simply one proposal. However, your aim is still to persuade your audience that the plan you are advocating is well thought out and likely to be effective.

Topping and tailing

You have now structured the bulk of your presentation – all your groups of paper slips should fit under one of these four headings: position, problem, possibilities or proposal – and you're pretty well ready to sit down and start writing.

There are just two more pieces of the jigsaw to include in the presentation: the beginning and the end. You need to sandwich the four Ps between an opening and closing gambit, a hello and a good-bye. These are the verbal equivalent of the title page, the objective and so on which you included in your report in the last chapter.

The hello can be a few simple sentences, in which you welcome people and thank them for attending your presentation. If there is anyone present who doesn't know you, you should introduce yourself. Say why you are giving the presentation – your objective. And you should also give people an indication of what to expect – just as a guide tells the group that the trek through the jungle will take three days and will be very hot, and that they should expect to get bitten by mosquitos. You should say how long the presentation will last, what form it will take and whether to ask questions during it or afterwards.

You can wind up the presentation in a sentence or two; you should simply thank them for listening and invite questions if that is the format you're following. But if you don't give any indication that you've finished, other than your silence, people can be left unsure for a moment of whether there may be more to come. So always give your presentation a clear, polite ending.

Writing

You know exactly what points you're going to make and in what order. Now it's just a matter of filling it out with words. And the first question for many people is: should you use a script? The answer is an absolute no; a script will come across as stilted and uncomfortable in a small group. Reading to your audience from a script (or reciting verbatim from memory) is also somehow insulting. Why drag them along to a presentation for a script you could have posted or e-mailed? A presentation audience – especially a small audience – expects the personal touch from you.

But how can you be sure of saying what you want to, and sticking to the structure we've just established, if you're talking off the top of your head? You can't. And it is equally insulting to drag your audience along and then give them a disordered selection of information from which some points are inadvertently left out, and others are included at confusing moments.

So you can't have a script and you're not supposed to present without a script. But, paradoxical though these conditions might seem, there is in fact a third way. Give your presentation from notes. You're not reading from a script, but you have a reminder to ensure that you stay on track and include everything the audience wants to hear.

Creating notes

So how do you prepare the notes? Well, the best way is to write the speech out in full, and then condense it down. Make sure you write your script in spoken rather than written English; they aren't the same thing. Even though you will condense your script into notes, it tends to be hard to abandon your original tone, so it's important to get it right from the start. Keep it chatty, and use phrases and expressions you would employ when talking at a meeting, for example. If you're presenting to your superiors, use the language of deference in your script: 'You will know better than I do . . . ', 'I'm sure you will have considered this . . . ' and so on.

It can help to script your presentation by dictating what you want to say into a dictaphone, working from your notes on slips of paper, ordered according to the four Ps structure. Type up this version of the presentation and then work on the manuscript it has given you: reorder anything that you feel needs it, take time to think up the best examples and analogies, and add any particularly clear or useful phrases you come up with.

When you turn this script back into notes, they will probably be very similar to your original key points which you wrote on your slips of paper. You will, however, have added any special phrases or examples you want to use and you may well have added headings, underlinings and so on to help you find your way around the notes easily. I find it helps to write notes on index cards. They are easy to hold and if you're a bit shaky it doesn't show as much as with a large, thin sheet of paper. It is also far less obtrusive than a sheaf of A4 paper. Start each new section, or sub-section if you like, on a fresh index card and staple or tag the whole lot together in the corner so that they can't get out of order if you happen to drop them.

There's one other ingredient you need to include in a presentation script: signposts. When you read a report (or anything else) you unconsciously look ahead to see how long a particular section is, or you notice that there are three points written under a particular heading, or you know that the next section is going to explain the bits you don't understand at the moment, because you've seen the heading.

Your presentation audience doesn't have this luxury. They have no idea how long you're going to go on for, or what's coming next, or whether the point you're making now is one of two points or the first of 17 . . . unless you tell them. And if you don't tell them, they'll spend as much time trying to work it out as they will listening to you.

So keep them posted. Each time you reach the end of a section, say so. Intersperse your presentation with remarks like:

➤ 'So that's the situation we're in at present. Now let's look briefly at the reasons why we need to change . . . '

➤ 'I'll explain the three options these trial results indicate and then we'll look at which is the best one . . . '

➤ 'I'm going to outline the benefits and the drawbacks of each option . . . '

Visual aids

Visual aids are there to support what you are saying. Make sure that each one adds impact, clarity, memorability or authority to what you are saying. If it doesn't, don't use it or it will distract the audience from the point you are making. A visual which is not for you is against you.

If you've attended many presentations you will know that at the end of the presentation, you are far more likely to remember one well conceived visual aid than 20 which simply repeated what the presenter was already saying. If you have only one point during the presentation when a visual aid is needed, only use one. Remember your objective; the aim of the exercise is to meet the objective, not to show off your fancy computer or impress people with the hours you must have spent preparing all those OHP slides.

Choosing your visuals

Once you have written your script, go through it asking yourself where the audience would benefit from an illustration or an explanation of a point. Sometimes, for example, a simple graph can add clarity and replace 500 words of verbal explanation. But only a simple graph can do this; never flash up a visual of a complex chart or graph – redesign it so that it draws attention to a trend or a comparison, don't include every figure and blip.

Sometimes a photograph or a line illustration can clearly show a piece of equipment or a product with which your audience is not familiar, and which they would take precious minutes to grasp from a verbal description alone.

These are the kind of visuals you should be looking for – the ones which can do something valuable for the presentation which you cannot achieve, or not so effectively, without them. A visual aid should add one of the following:

➤ *Impact*. Try asking yourself what single point you most want your audience to take away from the presentation, and then design a memorable visual aid which reinforces it. You can use more than one impact visual in a presentation, of course, but by definition too many of them would dilute the effect of each one.

➤ *Clarity*. Many visual aids help to explain something that might otherwise be unclear. Charts and graphs fall into this category, but they must be simple representations; the detailed figures should be given out later, if they are needed at all. Photographs and illustrations are usually far better than a description of something the audience has never seen.

> *Memorability.* A visual aid is always worthwhile if it helps people remember an important point. A product demonstration is more effective for this reason, among others. Often, handing round a simple piece of equipment or a product prototype helps to fix it in people's minds. If you want your audience to know what went into the mailpack for the trial campaign, don't try to explain it; just give them each a mailpack – and let them open it for themselves.

> *Authority.* Some things are hard to believe unless you can see them with your own eyes. If you want to impart something to your audience which they may not believe, use a visual to support your assertions. Perhaps you're insisting that the printer can produce really good quality brochures with their new equipment, despite what the incredibly low price might suggest. Don't just tell them – show them. Bring along some samples so they can see for themselves.

Delivery

It's impossible to teach delivery effectively in a book; it's something that needs to be done face-to-face. The best way to learn it is by practising in front of a mirror, into a microphone or dictaphone and with friends or colleagues who will give you honest and constructive criticism.

However, there are some points worth making on the printed page, if only because they give you guidelines to follow and errors to watch out for when you come to practise. And the key to all of them is to try to behave as if you weren't giving a presentation, but simply chatting naturally to colleagues – as if you were making an extended point at a meeting, for example. This means that you are not trying to learn any new techniques, but simply to remove the overlay of false mannerisms that we all mysteriously and pointlessly acquire when we know we are giving a presentation.

For this reason, I can't give you a list of things to do when you speak in a presentation, but only a list of things to avoid doing. So here is a checklist of the chief mannerisms to avoid when you stand in front of a group of colleagues in order to explain something to them without interruption.

➤ *Mumbling.* Don't risk speaking too quietly; it's better to be a little on the loud side. Imagine you're holding a conversation with the person sitting furthest from you and pitch your volume accordingly.

➤ *Gabbling.* It's better to speak too slowly than too quickly. In fact, if the adrenalin is flowing you will always speak faster than you think, so take this into account.

➤ *Hesitating.* A presentation full of 'ums' and 'ers' generally only afflicts people who haven't rehearsed enough. So long as you prepare thoroughly you shouldn't have to worry about this one.

➤ *Swallowing words.* The most commonly swallowed words are the ends of sentences, which can be dropped to the point of becoming inaudible. So make sure you keep the interest in your voice right to the last word of each sentence.

➤ *Repetitive mannerisms.* The audience will be distracted if you constantly fiddle with your cuffs or your hair, or adopt verbal catchphrases such as 'you know what I mean?' Used in moderation, it is better to ignore these than to get hung up on them; but if you use them excessively, you will need to learn to avoid them.

➤ *Poor eye contact.* Look at everyone as you would in normal conversation, making sure you include everyone, even those sitting right at the edge or the back. Don't stare, but don't avoid eye contact.

Writing reports

 Honing Your Deadly Skills: **Writing reports, like giving presentations, is a central form of communication for managers and also one on which you will be judged by your bosses. And that's not the only similarity: a report is really a written presentation and many of the techniques of writing an effective, impressive report are the same as for giving a persuasive, polished presentation.**

There are five key stages in preparing and writing a report:

1   planning;

2   research;

3   structuring;

4   writing;

5   visual presentation.

The first three stages – planning, research and structuring – are exactly the same as they are for presentations. Planning means setting your objective in exactly the same way, and scheduling your time to make sure the report gets the time it needs. You should research it in just the same way, collecting all your pieces of information and writing them on slips of paper. And the structure is the same, following the four Ps.

It's worth mentioning, however, that there are some reports that don't include any kind of proposal. These are information-only reports, such as the monthly management report, for example. There is no set structure for these – you simply take the groups into which you sorted your slips of paper at the end of the research process and put them in to the most logical order you can find. This might be date order, chronological order, by department, by region, by product – it depends entirely on the subject of the report. Just make sure that the order makes the most sense it can.

Writing

We looked at the general skills of writing clear, readable English in Chapter 2. However, there are some additional points worth making about reports. Most reports are designed not only to inform but also to persuade, so it is in your interests to get the reader on your side with the clearest, most easy-to-read style you can.

Put yourself in the reader's shoes and try to write in the style that suits them. Most of the time, this is probably your own natural style, but it might not be. If your report is intended for the board of directors and they are all old fuddy-duddies educated at public schools, you'll probably impress them more if you follow slightly more old-fashioned rules of grammar than usual. You don't have to become one of them, but at least steer clear of starting sentences with 'And . . . ', and find out what split infinitives are so that you can avoid using them.

Use examples and analogies

You can also make your report easier to read if you use plenty of examples to illuminate any points which might not be clear otherwise. Instead of simply saying: 'Direct mail gives a scope which advertising can't for using eye-catching shapes', add an example: 'In the trial campaign, we sent out one leaflet printed on card cut out in the shape of a front door, with a flap for the letterbox.'

If you think a concept might be unclear, use an analogy to explain it. Your readers don't have the opportunity they would in a conversation to ask for clarification, so you need to be sure that you explain everything they could possibly want to know. An analogy is one of those explanations which begins 'It's a bit like . . . ' or 'It's as if . . . '. For example, if you want to explain how direct mail compares with press advertising, you could say 'It's like walking up to people in the street and talking to them, instead of just standing at the side of the road wearing a sandwich board.'

No jargon or clichés

Make sure your readers can understand and take in everything you say. Don't use jargon – which you can define as anything your readers don't understand. The word 'software' is jargon to someone who knows nothing about computers.

And avoid clichés, too, because they slide past the reader without any meaning being absorbed. We're all so used to seeing phrases like 'meeting customers' needs' that we no longer take them in. What is the alternative, you may wonder? The answer is to quote hard facts: 'Customer satisfaction has increased from 83 per cent to 94 per cent in the areas where the trial was held.'

Pick your words

Your choice of words will affect the readability of your report. Be as simple and as factual as possible. Use active rather than passive verbs, because they are much easier to read and keep the pace moving along. A passive verb is one where something is done to the subject of the sentence; where the verb is active, the subject performs the action.

So 'The staff were encouraged to make suggestions' is passive. The active version is 'We encouraged the staff to make suggestions'.

By the same token, concrete nouns make your writing far easier to follow and take in than abstract ones. A concrete noun is one to which you can attach a visual picture: 'transportation' is abstract, 'car' is concrete. 'Communication' is abstract, a 'phone call' is concrete.

Accuracy

It is important to make sure that your use of English is accurate. By all means use a computer spellcheck or a grammar check, but not if it dissuades you from checking thoroughly by eye. Computer spelling and grammar checks don't pick up everything. If you misspell a word in a way which forms another word, your spellcheck will accept it even though it's wrong. For example, if you miss the letter 'd' off the end of the word 'and', you are left with 'an', which is still a word (and it may not be the right one).

So double check your spelling, grammar and punctuation. And if you are not a natural at such things, get someone else to check it for you too. If it's an important report, get someone else to read it anyway; it's always difficult to do an accurate check of something you've written yourself. You know what it says, so the eye tends to skim slightly, and can therefore miss mistakes that someone else, reading it for the first time, would pick up.

Visual presentation

You have now all but completed your report. The final stage in preparing it involves adding a few finishing touches and then laying it out visually to maximize readability.

Topping and tailing

You've written the main body of the report, but most reports need a few additional features added – none of them difficult – which will help the readers to follow the report or give them useful extra information. Almost all reports need the following:

➤ title page, including the author's name (this means you) and the date;

➢ contents page;

➢ page numbers;

➢ a summary (we'll look at this in a moment);

➢ an appendix or appendices.

You might also need to include in your report a glossary, a bibliography, a list of sources, useful addresses or contacts and acknowledgements.

The summary

The only ingredient in the topping and tailing which should require any explanation is the summary. Any report which runs to more than three or four pages should include a summary. This goes at the beginning and should be between a paragraph and a page long. It should never go over the page. It needs to be there for

➢ anyone who doesn't have time to read the full report;

➢ anyone who wants to recap quickly on the report sometime after reading it, for example as a reminder just before going into a meeting at which the report will be discussed.

Since this is its function, it obviously needs to say everything that the full report says, only more briefly; it summarizes the report. It needs no supporting data or arguments – these are in the report. It needs to contain only the bare facts.

Layout

There's a world of difference between trying to plough your way through pages of close-typed text with no breaks and reading a document with plenty of white page showing between the lines, and never more than a couple of paragraphs before you reach a heading or sub-heading. Layout can make your readers' hearts sink or their spirits rise when they open your report. So here's how to ensure the latter:

➢ Double space and leave comfortable margins.

➢ Use headings and sub-headings.

➢ Use lists.

➤ Keep it simple. Never mind if your word processing package has a 150 different fonts. This isn't a design showcase, it's a report. Use no more than two typefaces – one for text and one for headings. And keep the style of headings simple, don't have a huge selection of type sizes, capitals, underlined words, bold words – just pick the simplest ones you can and no more than you really need. It will only distract from what you're saying.

Summary

Clear, succinct and well-thought-out communications with senior management are a vital part of running a successful department and boosting your personal career prospects. There are four key routes to winning the ear of senior management:

➤ identifying the best lines of communication upwards;

➤ making your point at meetings;

➤ giving internal presentations;

➤ writing reports.

Identifying the best lines of communication

If your communication line upwards to top management is blocked at any point, you need to:

➤ Identify the problem.

- find the weak point;
- establish the nature of the obstruction.

➤ Deal with the problem.

- put everything in writing;
- clear the blockage; or
- overcome the obstruction.

Making your point at meetings

If you want to get your point across in meetings you should limit yourself to making a few well prepared and argued key points: less is more.

➤ Decide what you want to say in advance.

➤ Work out the best way to express it, with most impact.

➤ Get the chairperson on your side.

Giving internal presentations

There are six stages to follow in order to produce effective, persuasive presentations:

1 planning;

2 research;

3 structuring;

4 writing;

5 visual aids;

6 delivery.

Writing reports

A report is rather like a presentation which has been written down. There are five key stages in writing a clear report which will impress your bosses:

1 planning;

2 research;

3 structuring;

4 writing;

5 visual presentation.

Here's a quick checklist to recap the key points about your writing style:

➤ write in the style the reader will prefer to read;

➤ use plenty of examples and analogies to illustrate what you're saying;

> avoid jargon;

> avoid clichés;

> use active, not passive, verbs;

> use concrete, not abstract, nouns.

The Fifth Deadly Skill

Communicating with the Team

For many middle or senior managers the team is really a department or section consisting of a number of teams. Nevertheless, to communicate effectively with this group of people you have to treat them in the same way as team leaders treat individual teams. In other words, you have to engender a strong and positive group identity and a sense of collective purpose among the individuals who make up your team.

Good communication with the team, therefore, is not only about giving and receiving information, but also about doing it in a way which reinforces the team's identity, and its members' commitment to the team's objectives. This chapter is about how to communicate with groups of team members or even the whole team or department collectively, and to create and build team spirit in the process. This kind of communication generally happens in one of three ways:

➤ team briefings;

➤ meetings;

➤ training.

It is also essential that you send out the right messages to your team by presenting a consistent attitude in all your dealings with your team members, so that each communication reinforces all the others.

Team briefing

One of the keys to good communication within organizations is team briefing, a system which was pioneered by The Industrial Society. The idea is that all managers and team leaders, from the very top down, are briefed regularly and, in turn, brief their own teams so that the briefings cascade, as it were, down the organization giving a direct line of communication right through the company.

The team briefing system first developed from a recognition of three basic principles about communication:

➤ It isn't possible for people to co-operate fully if they don't know what's going on.

➤ The most effective way to bond a team together is to talk to it as a team about things which are important to the team.

➤ A team leader's position of authority is reinforced without confrontation by the fact that they give briefings.

A properly run team briefing system has a huge number of benefits for the individuals, the team and the organization as a whole.

➤ It reduces industrial problems because staff understand the reasons behind changes.

➤ It increases company loyalty.

➤ It consolidates the position of team leaders.

➤ It helps resolve problems because, once the staff understand them, often they can provide solutions which management alone would never have found.

➤ It increases staff morale.

 Honing Your Deadly Skills: **Team briefing is one of the most valuable methods there is of communicating effectively with your team and, as they become used to it, your team members will appreciate being kept in the picture about where they're coming from and where they're going.**

If team briefing is going to work, it needs the commitment of top management. A team briefing system which fails is worse for company morale than one which never existed, so if you're going to do it, do it properly. Make time for briefing sessions, make them regular with dates set well in advance and make sure everyone is there. If you treat the briefings seriously, so will the staff and they will want to be there. Make sure it's understood that they are expected to attend and shouldn't make other appointments which clash; only on very rare occasions should anyone need to miss a briefing session.

Running the briefing session

The Industrial Society has established five rules, all of which must be followed if team briefing is to work effectively. The briefing sessions must be:

1   face-to-face;

2   in teams of between four and 15 people;

3   run by the team leader – the most senior person in the group;

4   regular (monthly is usually about right);

5   relevant to the team.

Certain subjects for discussion will have come down from the top of the organization through managers' briefing sessions and will be discussed by some or all teams. Others will be specific to a single team. Before each briefing, the team leader should determine what topics will be covered.

Team briefing sessions should last for about half an hour. The best times to hold them are on a regular day of the week soon after everyone starts work, such as Monday mornings at 9.30, or even over a departmental lunch. The Industrial Society recommends that you have four categories of information on which you brief your team – the four Ps:

1   *Progress.* Give the team its performance results. Did it meet last month's targets? How does it compare with other teams in the organization, or with competitors? What new orders have there been? Have they had any special successes or failures? Have the competition brought out any new products?

2   *Policy.* This sections covers any changes in systems, deadlines, holiday arrangements, legislation which affects the team, training courses, pensions and so on.

3   *People*. This section briefs team members about any new team members, any members who are leaving (including why, and where they're going), a new MD or changes in senior management, changes in other departments the team deals with, promotions (including why), overtime, relocation, absenteeism, exhibition stand staffing and so on.

4   *Points for action*. The fourth section covers information which team members may have to act on: practical information such as new security measures that must be taken, maintenance priorities, correcting rumours, housekeeping details and so on.

A brief is just that – a brief; it's not a discussion. You have set your agenda in advance and you should work through it.

➤   Encourage questions, but don't get into discussions or debates. By all means fill people in with more information, explanations or reasons if they want them, but don't get into arguments. If you think an argument is brewing, explain that this is not the place, but let people know that they can raise the issue another time.

➤   Encourage comments and suggestions and make a note of them, but don't discuss them right now. You can always fix up an individual or team session later to go through them.

➤   If anyone asks a question you don't know the answer to, find it out for them in the next day or two.

➤   Make sure that team members have understood anything complicated by asking questions to check they are clear.

➤   Summarize the key points at the end of the briefing.

➤   Find something positive to finish with so that people leave on an upbeat.

➤   Don't run over time – 30 minutes should be ample.

➤   Give out the date of the next briefing and get everyone to mark it in their diary so they can make sure they are free.

➤   If anyone is absent from the briefing session, brief them yourself when they return.

Training and monitoring

Before you introduce a team briefing system, you should first train all your team leaders to run the system effectively. (We'll look at training later in this chapter.) They cannot possibly be expected to run briefings unless you communicate to them properly what you want them to do, how you want them to do it and what you want them to achieve. But the very best training is for them to see you doing things right in your own team briefings to them and their colleagues.

Once you have trained your team leaders and got your briefing sessions up and running, you should monitor them occasionally to make sure they are still running effectively. So if you brief several of your people, who then go on to brief their own teams, you will need to:

➤ check what information of their own they are adding to your brief, in order to make it more specific to their own team;

➤ attend their briefing sessions from time to time (but only as an observer);

➤ make random checks from time to time with their team members to see how effective their briefing has been.

You should carry out regular and continual monitoring to be sure the system is still working effectively, and that there are no Chinese whispers getting into the system.

 Honing Your Deadly Skills: **The Industrial Society produces its own material on team briefing, based on nearly 30 years' experience, including books, videos and an information pack. You can contact The Industrial Society at: Peter Runge House, 3 Carlton House Terrace, London SW1Y 5DG. Tel: 0171 479 1000**

Meetings

We've already seen, in Chapter 3, that a meeting has three possible functions: to inform, discuss or decide. And we also touched on the social benefits of meetings, which are an important part of cementing group identity, helping people to recognize their own contribution and encouraging a feeling of commitment to any decisions made by the group.

Meetings are a particularly important part of team communication, because they are a formalized coming together of individuals within the team. The way team meetings work will have a huge impact on the way the team works outside the meeting. Team members will take the style and tone of your meetings away with them and apply them to the rest of their work. If meetings are places of conflict and heated disagreement, this will be reflected in the way their members work generally. Equally, if your meetings are places of co-operation and collective focus, so will the rest of the workplace be.

It's worth establishing a set of ground rules for effective team meetings which any team leaders working under you should also follow:

1   The respect the team shows for its meetings demonstrates the commitment its members have to the team. So you need to adopt a formal style for running meetings, even if the atmosphere is informal. Decisions made by half a dozen colleagues over a lunchtime drink just don't carry the weight of the same decisions made by the same people sitting round a table, without interruptions and circulating minutes afterwards. So everyone should give priority to turning up to meetings on time and all meetings should have proper agendas, minutes and so on.

2   It's important that everyone should be involved in regular team meetings and in any meetings about really vital issues. They won't feel they have a stake in the decisions coming out of the meeting if they weren't present at it and contributing to it.

3   If your team holds project meetings, put a different person in the chair each time. This helps to play down the hierarchy and helps to impress on the people that they are not working for any one person, but for the team and its objectives.

4   Encourage effective meetings by training everyone in your team to follow the same set of guidelines:

> ➤ Always ask for clarification if you don't understand anything fully; by the same token, expect to repeat or explain anything patiently and willingly if other members of the team ask you to.

➤ Everyone should be conscious of encouraging quieter members of the team to offer their views.

➤ Listen to each other and allow every idea to be aired and treated with respect and fairness.

5   Make sure that any really important decisions are always made with a consensus. This doesn't mean a unanimous vote in favour, nor a majority vote (where the minority can be strongly against). A consensus decision is one that everyone can live with, even if it's not everyone's first choice, because only if *everyone* is prepared to support the decision will they all be fully committed to seeing it through. You need to explain to everyone in the team the importance of consensus, and you need to establish in advance which decisions call for a consensus. Once your team members appreciate the need for it they will manage to arrive at it, even if it takes a little longer than otherwise.

Your job as chairperson

As chair you are responsible of course for agendas and minutes, keeping meetings to time and establishing action points – all important skills but ones which there isn't room to cover in detail here. (They are, however, covered in one of the companion books in this series, *The Seven Deadly Skills of Management*.) At the moment, we are concerned with the techniques of making the most effective use of team meetings, in a way which gets results and bonds the group together.

As a manager, you have the key role in the meetings you chair. Your behaviour will determine whether the meeting is effective or not. Both good and bad meetings are a direct reflection on the chair. It is very tempting to see the job of chairing a meeting as an opportunity to wield power, impose decisions, air opinions, or establish authority. But these are not the means of achieving a good result from the meeting. It is important to be aware of the reasons why you are holding the meeting. People will not feel they share responsibility for decisions if they don't feel they had their say at the meeting, but merely that you called everyone together in order to impose your views on them. They will not say what they think if they fear your criticism. They will not discuss their opinions openly if they know they will be shouted down, by you or anyone else.

In order for the meeting to achieve its aims, you must adopt the right attitude in the chair. And the key to this is to recognize that while you may be the boss outside the meeting, as chair you are the servant of the group, not its master. You are there to make things run smoothly and help the meeting along. Your job is to hold focus, clarify, explain, keep the discussion moving along and ensure that it arrives at the best possible resolution in the shortest possible time.

You should avoid making any intervention which is more than a sentence or two long. If you express your own view, especially early on in discussions, junior members of the team may resist expressing an opposite view for fear of contradicting the boss. It is much better to be seen as neutral, at least until enough debate has taken place to convince you one way or the other. Your neutrality is important because the members of the meeting will see you as the servant of the group – your interests are the interests of the group, so you are on everyone's side. This makes discipline far easier to enforce if necessary – and it is necessary far less often.

Keeping control

You are aiming to run your meetings efficiently and effectively, so you want to make sure that every item is dealt with in the most logical way for maximum speed and to make sure that everyone in the team understands it and has their say. So you need a structure and you need to adhere to it.

There is a logical route to take through every agenda item to ensure this. Sometimes you may be able to omit one or two stages; for example, if everyone is in agreement you won't need to justify the facts. Or if you are only discussing ideas at this stage you won't need to make a decision at the end of the item (although you will still need to agree the next action to take). There are five key stages, which you should progress through in order, even if you skip over one or two of them.

1   *Establish the facts.* Either you or the person responsible for the item should open the subject with a brief introduction to establish the facts. The introduction should explain:

➢ the reason for the item being on the agenda;
➢ a brief summary of the history of the subject bringing it up to the current position;

➤ what needs to be established, decided or resolved;
➤ the key arguments on both sides;
➤ the possible courses of action.

2   *State the evidence.* The next thing to do is to go through the evidence which backs up the facts. If this is at all lengthy, it should have been circulated in advance – or if the topic is controversial. If people don't have the chance to study controversial information in advance, they are likely to feel that someone is trying to get the better of them by depriving them of the chance to prepare properly. This is exactly the kind of feeling which is damaging to team morale.

3   *Discuss what the evidence means.* Now you can open up the discussion. Everyone knows what they are talking about, and to what end, so this is the time to invite views and arguments about the conclusions which you can draw from the evidence.

4   *Arrive at a conclusion.* Once views have all been discussed and opinions aired, it's time to progress to some kind of conclusion. The discussion should now move towards establishing some kind of consensus view. It is your job to remind people what the aim of the meeting is – to put forward ideas, to reach a decision, to agree the outline for a proposal or whatever – and to steer them towards doing this.

5   *Make a decision based on that conclusion.* Once a conclusion has been reached, you should summarize it for everyone's benefit, and then record it, together with any action points arising as a result.

As chair of the meeting, you must make sure that the group follows this route through every agenda item. If they try to do things out of order, keep them in line with a firm: 'Hold on. Let's finish establishing the facts first before we start discussing them' or 'We've all had a chance to argue our case; let's move on now. We need to decide whether we should cut down our trade show attendance.'

Keep firm control of the meeting and pull the discussion back on course as soon as you see it start to wander. Don't let people ramble for five minutes about their past trade show experiences before you stop them, or they'll all think they have five minutes' grace before being brought back to the discussion. Don't intimidate people; stop them with a grin if you can. Simply be firm, brief and neutral – you're on the side of effective debate on the subject.

You should intervene – briefly – if you think anything needs clarifying, or if you want to invite a contribution from someone whose ideas or experience you think would be useful, especially quieter or more junior members of the team who may be nervous of offering their view. Sometimes an interim summary is helpful in a complex debate, to reiterate the points you have established so far, and any points of consensus, particularly if you sense that anyone is getting confused.

Dealing with difficult people

It's much easier to maintain control if your meetings always contain a group of pleasant, easy-going people who get on well together even if they do have occasional disagreements. And the better run your team is, and the more effective your communications with its members are, the more likely it is that your meetings will be friendly and co-operative. However, not all meetings fall into this category, even in the best run teams. A good chair will still maintain control of the meeting if there are difficult people present, but it does require you to master some additional, more sophisticated communication techniques.

Get everyone on the same side

The first thing you need to do to keep a potentially fiery meeting under control is to unite everyone as a team behind the cause of solving the problem or reaching the decision. They may have opposing views, but you want them to express them with a single, collective objective.

So you should be especially vigilant in the techniques we've seen so far:

➤ focus the team on finding a resolution;

➤ establish the facts;

➤ don't take sides;

➤ don't allow digressions, especially not any which dredge up past disagreements.

You will also find that if the discussion is heated, there are two other specific techniques which help to defuse things:

➤ *Don't ignore people's emotions.* If you drive them underground they are more likely to erupt far worse later on. Allow people to let off steam first, acknowledge their feelings (without taking sides) and then encourage them to calm down. If someone is clearly angry, ask them to say how they feel: 'You sound a bit angry. What's the problem?' Don't let others interrupt, but allow the person to express their feelings. If necessary, allow others to do the same. Then move on: 'I think it's a help to get everyone's feelings out in the open, but let's not get into a slanging match. Now we all understand the feelings involved in this issue, let's get down to looking at the problem objectively.'

➤ *Bring in other people.* If two people are trying to slug it out across the table, you can help defuse things by getting other, less emotionally involved members of the team to contribute. This broadens the debate and helps to calm down the aggressive participants while they listen to the comments of those they are not in conflict with. Don't change the subject; just invite a different perspective. Ask other people questions which will indicate the extent of the problem, or put it in perspective, or help to identify the cause of it.

 Honing Your Deadly Skills: **You will find that these techniques, along with all the others we have looked at, will enable you to deal with any problem types at team meetings: the quiet ones, the abusive ones, the ones who always ramble and so on. The combination of these techniques, once you have mastered them, will keep any meeting under control and will create a co-operative and motivated team which is focused on collective objectives.**

Training

Training is a highly effective way to communicate with your staff. Not only can you teach all the skills and impart all the information that you want them to know, but by doing it you will be communicating other messages too. Training people tells them:

> that they are important to you;

> that they are worth investing in;

> that you believe they have the potential to learn new skills.

Training people motivates them because the new skills they learn give them the opportunity to take on new challenges and responsibilities.

It's useful to train people in working groups or teams, because this helps to reinforce the group. Everyone has to expose their weaknesses, and they will all identify potential in each other which they hadn't recognized before. Training as a team also encourages everyone to apply the lessons of training when they return to work. They all know what the others learnt, and they will encourage and remind each other.

What sort of training?

You can train your people in anything from practical skills such as mastering a new computer program, to interpersonal skills such as how to make meetings more effective. Everyone in the team needs to have their own, individual, training programme and you'll need to produce another training programme for the team as a whole, for such things as meetings skills. Whatever you do, don't use the lazy manager's dodge of seeing what courses are running and then seeing who you could send on them. This is a complete waste of time and the trainees know it. Your training programme must be geared to what training is needed, not what training is easily available. This doesn't mean, of course, that external courses are necessarily wrong – sometimes they are the best way to train a particular person in a particular skill – but you should choose them for the right reasons.

> Consider what skills it would be useful for each person to have, both practical and behavioural (such as time management).

> Then ask each team member to tell you what areas they think they need to be trained in, or would like to develop so they can handle new responsibilities in future.

This process should enable you to draw up a practical and challenging training programme, within your budget and time constraints, for each member of your team.

As well as individual training programmes, you'll also need to think through any collective skills which the team as a whole needs to learn. These should include teamwork skills, but will also include all sorts of other skills from exhibition planning to customer care, depending on the function and abilities of the team.

Training needs to be a fairly frequent activity for people to feel that they are being nurtured and encouraged, so put together training programmes which ensure that everyone has some kind of official training at least once a month, whether it is a three-day course or a one-hour team training session.

Internal or external training?

It's well worth mixing different types of training in the programme you draw up; it is more interesting and therefore more stimulating for the trainee. What's more, particular types of training are better for certain skills, so you will need to offer variety if you pick the best training method each time. In-house courses tend to be more suitable for training in subjects that deal with your organization's products or services, or its systems. If you want everyone in the team to use the same system for inducting new staff, or to learn the same guidelines for handling customer complaints, you'll need to train them in-house. You can always employ outside trainers to run in-house courses for you. Or you may not need a trainer at all – if you run a sales team for example, inviting one of your own organization's buyers along for a session can be very valuable.

Outside courses are better for learning universal skills such as time management, or for professional updates on new legislation. Residential courses and outward bound courses can be extremely good for bonding team members together, since they will socialize together in the evenings as well. This is especially useful if there are several new team members who haven't yet got to know each other well. As a general rule, if you need to train several team members in the same skill you should try to train them together, either in-house or externally, because the shared experience will help them to feel more like part of the same team.

And then there are all sorts of ways to train people informally, such as team crisis planning sessions, on-the-job training, job swapping, one-to-one sessions, videos and interactive training such as CD-ROM. One of the most useful ways to train the team as a whole is to organize group sessions to analyse how the team could do better, sometimes inviting customers – internal or external – to join you. Give the session a broad theme such as how to improve procedures, or how to build stronger relationships with other departments, and let the participants take it from there.

Following up the training

If you don't follow up training sessions, you undermine the messages you communicate by giving training in the first place. Failure to review training signals that you don't care how the trainee felt about the training or whether it was effective. And if you don't follow up the training you won't know whether it was useful, so how will you know whether it's worth using that course or that type of session in the future?

So you must always hold a review session a couple of weeks after training, to check that the team member has understood the lessons and is now incorporating them into their job. If several people – or the whole team – took part in the training you should review the training with the group. If you do this and you feel that anyone has had special difficulties learning or applying the training, you can also hold a separate session with them individually.

There's one more crucial point about training: if you teach someone a new skill, you must make sure they have a chance to use it. It is incredibly demoralizing to be taught, for example, how to give a presentation if you are never subsequently asked to give one. So if you're not going to give people the chance to use their new skills, don't train them in the first place. Some people resist training because they see it as a kind of covert criticism; you'll have to train them because they are useless at the moment, is the message they think other people will pick up.

Of course, training is actually very positive as we've seen: it should be seen as a compliment to the person that you think they are worth investing in and that with a bit more training they will be able to take on greater responsibilities or more difficult tasks. It's your job to make sure that this is your employees' attitude to training, but you'll have a hard time convincing them of it if you don't give them new challenges to meet once they have learnt the skills to cope with them.

Training is a promise to your team that you will increase the value of their contribution – don't break your promise.

Teamwork training

An important part of your job in communicating effectively with the team involves training them to maximize the best communication between themselves. Teams whose members communicate well with each other work far more effectively and happily than teams whose members don't. So you need to train the whole team in communication skills: you have to teach them to work as a team. The skills involved will help them to minimize conflict, which is one of the greatest enemies of good communication. The most common causes of conflict between team members are:

1   One person (or group) feels they are doing an unfair share of the work. This may be true or it may not; either way it needs dealing with. The problem generally stems from people believing that they are doing more than they should have to, or or that they have been given tasks that are less inspiring, important or valuable than everyone else's. Sometimes one person feels that another is getting the credit for the hard work which they themselves put in.

2   One person or group feels excluded from team discussions, consultations or decisions.

3   There is a straightforward personality clash.

Each of these problems calls for a different set of teamwork skills and everyone in the team will need to understand the steps which are needed to resolve the problem.

Unfair workload

➤   Everyone in the team should recognize that the aim is to meet the team's objectives effectively. Tasks are distributed in the way which best exploits everyone's strengths and maximizes the team's performance. So if the most effective way to get the job done sometimes involves helping out with a task which has been allocated to someone else, everyone should be willing to co-operate.

➢ Everyone should help to make sure that tasks are allocated fairly, in terms of the workload and its interest. There are some tasks that everyone hates; the team should make sure it isn't always the same person who gets lumbered with them. It's important not only that no one is unfairly loaded with work, but also that no one *feels* they are. If anyone does have a grudge about their workload, they should air it, preferably as soon as the task is given to them.

Feeling of exclusion

➢ Everyone should be permitted and encouraged, by you and by each other, to express a view about any aspect of the team's work, not only their own specific tasks. If the team is to work together as a unified group, people have to be involved in the group as a whole.

➢ All information which is relevant to the team and its work should be shared with everyone – not only the people whose work is directly affected.

➢ During team meetings and discussions, as we have already seen, people should be encouraged to ask for clarification on any point if they need it.

➢ There should be a team rule that no idea is sacred – if people have alternatives to suggest, or doubts about anything, they should voice them. All constructive criticisms, suggestions and ideas should be welcomed and treated with respect.

➢ Every time someone makes a suggestion, the rest of the group should hear them out before they start to disagree.

Personality clash

➢ Everyone in the team should understand that it is part of their job to minimize conflict between themselves and their colleagues. Encourage them to talk to each other directly when they feel unhappy with each other and not allow bad feeling to fester.

➢ Train everybody that the ends are more important than the means. There should be a joint focus on meeting objectives and targets and so long as these are achieved, it may be necessary to compromise on the means of achieving them.

➤ Team members should make a conscious effort to recognize each other's feelings, such as underconfidence, inexperience or stress, and support each other.

Members of a team which has been properly trained in teamwork skills will communicate far better with each other than they could without the training. But it is important that you refresh the training every so often so that they remember to apply it, especially if there are big changes in the team, or if anyone new joins.

Be consistent

You may present yourself as being fair, open and encouraging to all the members of your team at briefings, meetings and in training. But this kind of communication is hollow unless you follow it through in everything else you do. You should always make time to listen to genuine problems from people in the team, always encourage suggestions and ideas, and always give the impression that you view each individual as being important and having a valuable contribution to make to the team and to the organization.

Your good communications with the team will fail if you exhibit a tendency – even if only occasionally – to bawl people out in front of their colleagues, take sides at times of conflict, show favouritism, or cut people dead when you bump into them down at the shops on a Saturday. All these things will make it less likely that your employees will want to approach you when they have a brainwave about how the department can reduce its costs.

It's crucial to remember that to your team, you represent the organization. If you are dismissive, unapproachable and uninterested in their development, they will have a similar view of the organization as a whole. As we know, this will damage their morale and their loyalty to the organization, and these in turn will reduce their productivity. If, on the other hand, you are caring, encouraging and approachable, they will see the organization in a similar light and you will be responsible for their high levels of morale and loyalty to the company, and their concomitant higher productivity.

Summary

Whether you run a single team or a group of teams, your collective communications with the people who work for you will affect their morale and productivity. To get the best from your staff, you need to engender a strong team identity among them.

Team briefing

Every team leader from the top down should be briefed, and then go on to brief their own team. In order to work briefing sessions must be:

1   face-to-face;

2   in teams of between four and 15 people;

3   run by the team leader – the most senior person in the group;

4   regular (monthly is usually about right);

5   relevant to the team.

There are four categories of information on which to brief your team:

➤   progress;

➤   policy;

➤   people;

➤   points for action.

Meetings

Remember the key techniques for handling people:

➤   allow people to express their feelings and then move on;

➤   bring in other people;

➤   stick to facts;

➤   don't take sides;

➤   don't allow digressions;

➤   invite contributions from those who won't volunteer them;

➤ keep your own interventions brief;

➤ instil a sense that time is valuable and not to be wasted.

Training

In order to provide effective training to your team:

➤ Prepare an individual training programme for each person, in consultation with them.

➤ Prepare a team training programme for collective skills, and to communicate a sense of team unity.

➤ Vary internal, external, formal and informal training, and choose the most suitable approach for the type of training you are giving.

➤ Always follow up training with a review after about a fortnight.

➤ Train the whole team in teamwork skills.

Be consistent

Follow through your communication style in every encounter with your team members, at work and outside it. Be caring, approachable, encourage suggestions and ideas, and treat every individual as being important and valuable to the organization.

6

Communicating with the Individual

Whether the staff who report to you are junior staff or managers themselves, their loyalty and motivation will be hugely influenced by the way you communicate with them. And their attitude to you will influence their attitude to the whole organization.

This chapter is all about communicating one-to-one. The way you handle this key aspect of communication has a huge impact on individuals' motivation and this chapter looks at how you should approach people in order to encourage them to give their best.

Interviews are the times when you need to communicate formally on a one-to-one basis, and the key interviews where this counts are:

➢ selection;

➢ appraisal;

➢ discipline interviews;

➢ bad news interviews.

This chapter is not about the basic skills of how to conduct this kind of interview – which you presumably know already – but about how to use good communication skills to make the interview as effective as possible. The other important opportunity to communicate one-to-one is at induction, where you set the tone for the employee's attitude to the job and the organization for the future, so it's essential that you communicate effectively.

Motivation

Motivation is a huge subject, and one which encompasses factors ranging from money and status to job satisfaction and recognition. Not everyone is the same and not everyone is motivated by the same things. However, as far as one-to-one communication is concerned, there are certain factors which motivate just about everyone.

➤ The better people understand their own jobs, and how they fit into the rest of the organization, the more motivated they will be. They can see that what they do makes a difference to everyone else and affects the organization's performance. This is a point that should be reinforced regularly, not just explained once when they first start the job – keep showing them where their job fits in. Take them on a tour round the factory, or put them on an exhibition stand to meet customers if their own job rarely brings them into contact with them. And if their job is behind the scenes in the organization, show them the products in operation occasionally – take them to one of your retail outlets, or on a visit to a client to see the product working on site.

➤ Everyone should have clear targets which they help to set. These should stretch them, but shouldn't be unattainable. Sit down with each of your team and agree targets regularly. If people aren't clear what you want them to achieve, or feel they simply can't reach the target, they will be very demoralized. Equally, it is very demotivating for them to feel that you are giving them work they could do in their sleep – it implies that you think that's all they're capable of.

➤ People need to be involved in the department and the organization in order to care about what happens to it. So tell them everything you can and keep them informed about the company's performance. Encourage them to make suggestions and to put forward ideas and be seen to listen – if they feel their contributions are never appreciated, and their ideas are never taken up, they will stop volunteering them.

You can also make a huge impact on people's motivation by the way you behave towards them day-to-day. In the rest of this chapter we're going to look at interviews, but as a manager you need to adopt certain attitudes all the time – not only at interviews but even when you pass in the corridor – in order to motivate people to work their hardest for you.

Say what you mean

Don't send out messages which conflict with your words. If you say to someone 'You've done a great job on this exhibition stand' and then you start rearranging all the display materials, they won't believe what you will say, and they will be frustrated at your contradicting your own words. It's much better to say 'You've made a good start, but I think we could still improve it a little.' Then you're being honest, and they are clear.

Focus on ends, not means

Don't try to do people's jobs for them; it makes them wonder why they're there at all. If they are setting up an exhibition stand for you, give them a clear brief and let them decide how to meet it. That's what you employ them for. For example, tell them you want it bright and colourful, with lots of space to move around, an informal feel and with the focus on your new products. If you don't feel they've achieved this, don't start rearranging it, but restate the end objective. Explain that you don't feel the focus is strongly enough on the new products, and perhaps suggest they move around some of the display material and literature. Let *them* decide what to move and where to. If you take over, they'll feel like going home and leaving you to get on with it.

Be positive

If someone's work isn't up to scratch, don't give them the impression that you think they're hopeless; let them know that they have done well in some areas, but others still need a bit more attention to bring them up to the same standard. If you say: 'This report really isn't right at all. We'd better go through all the problems . . . ' you will demoralize them and make them feel that it's not worth trying again.

The positive approach is to start and end with a good point, and deal with the problems in between in a constructive way. For example:

'You did well to get this done at all with the workload we've had over the last couple of weeks. And you've really got the hang of how to structure a report. The information you're including is a bit confused, though, so I think we should go through it and see where you're having problems, so we can sort them out for next time . . . '
Then end on a positive note, for example, 'You've got a good eye for layout and presentation, haven't you? Your work always looks inviting to read.' Be specific, in your praise as well as your positive criticism. 'It's a good report' feels less like praise than 'Your layout is very good', because it is so vague it seems less genuine.

A similar approach applies to handling mistakes. If you're doing your job properly, and your staff are well motivated, their mistakes won't be the result of not caring. They do care, but if you treat them as though they don't, they will stop caring. Have you ever felt dreadful about a mistake and then been bawled out for it by your boss? The normal reaction is to feel that your boss doesn't credit you with enough loyalty or integrity to feel bad about making a mistake, so they'll have to *make* you feel bad. No, if your staff are well motivated – which is down to you – it's much better to say, 'I know you feel rotten, but we all make mistakes. Let's talk through how it happened, so we can make sure it doesn't happen again.'

This sets up a culture in which people feel happy to 'own up' to mistakes, knowing that they won't be hammered for it, which in turn means that problems are far less likely to get out of control through people trying to cover up their mistakes. You can help further by admitting to your own mistakes and relating stories about your past mistakes, so that people feel that mistakes should be avoided if possible, but don't have to be treated as punishable offences.

Be likeable

There is a popular myth that it doesn't matter whether your staff like you or not. In fact, it matters a lot. People are more motivated, learn faster and set themselves higher standards, if they work for a boss whom they like. This doesn't mean grovelling – you don't have to be everyone's best friend – and it doesn't mean you can't be firm when it's necessary. It just means being friendly and pleasant, fair-minded, honest and happy to give credit when it is deserved.

It also means being polite. Don't tell people what to do; ask them. If you've motivated your team properly they won't challenge or refuse you. Say 'please' and 'thank you' as you would with anyone else, and treat people as equals in human terms, even if their professional status isn't equal to yours. This applies especially if you ask anyone to do something which isn't their job: be clear that you know you are asking a favour, and be prepared to accept no for an answer. Say, for example: 'Keith, I know you're snowed under, but I could really do with someone phoning through to sales for this week's figures and Isobel isn't in today. Is there any chance you could do it?' If they say no, say: 'Fair enough, I'm sure I can find someone.' The odds are, though, that they will say yes because they know they aren't being taken for granted and that their co-operation will really be appreciated.

Be generous

Sooner or later, you'll need favours from people. You'll want someone to stay late to prepare for a big event, or people to come in at the weekend to help cope when the computer crashes, or someone to take over someone else's work when they go off sick. No one has to do these things, but you hope they'll say yes when you have to ask.

The way to maximize the likelihood of them co-operating is to be generous with them so that when you ask a favour they know you'd do the same for them – you probably already have. If it's remotely possible, be generous about giving people time off if there's a serious family problem, or letting them work at home occasionally if their childminder lets them down. The more prepared you are to be human, the less likely they are to take advantage of you.

Selection

Staff selection is a large subject, and we cannot go into all the skills involved here (they are covered more fully in the companion volume in this series, *The Seven Deadly Skills of Management*). In this section, we focus on just one important aspect of selection: the message you communicate to the candidates about the kind of organization they will be working for if they are offered (and accept) the job. This is a terribly important aspect of communication.

Honing Your Deadly Skills: **An organization is only as good as the people within it and if you want the best people to come and work for you, you need to communicate the best possible image of your organization to them when they apply for a job.**

First impressions

The moment the candidate sees your ad, they start to form an impression of your organization. So make sure it's a good one. A new appointment is a two-way thing: the candidates are vetting you as much as the other way round. Just imagine finding the perfect candidate, who you'd be proud to have as part of your organization, and offering them the job . . . only to have them turn it down because they don't really fancy working for you lot. So give the best possible impression from the start.

➤ Give all the important details – job title, objective and key responsibilities – as you can reasonably fit into the space without overcrowding it.

➤ Don't make generalizations; be specific. Give a salary range if you possibly can, don't just say 'attractive salary'. Likewise, don't waffle about 'good working conditions': if you want to mention them, state the hours, holiday entitlements or whatever it is you think will appeal.

➤ Give a brief description of your organization and what it does.

➤ Give the reader a clear course of action – a number to phone for an application form, or an address to write to, or whatever it is you want them to do.

➤ Give a closing date for applications.

Prepare

You need to present a professional image to each candidate and make them feel that you have taken trouble over their application and interview. Their attitude to you is important if you want them to accept the job if it's offered, or to speak well of your organization in future, even if they don't get the job.

You will also need to prepare in practical terms. If you realize too late that no one at reception knows the candidates are arriving and that the second chair in your office has been borrowed and you don't know where it has gone, and then your phone rings all the way through the interview, you'll give a dreadful impression to the candidates and you'll be so distracted you won't be able to concentrate on the interview. So think about these practical points:

➤ *Welcome the candidate.* Tell reception who is arriving and when, arrange for someone to greet them, decide where they will wait and prepare the area (make sure it is comfortable and leave copies of the annual report and customer newsletter there), make sure the candidate gets a chance to visit the cloakroom if they want to, and offer them a coffee or tea.

➤ *Prevent interruptions.* Divert your phone calls and make sure no one barges into the office. Have someone nearby stall any colleagues who want to interrupt you, or put a notice on the door.

➤ *Arrange the room.* Don't interview candidates across the barrier of a desk. Ideally you should both (and anyone else on the panel) be sitting in comfortable chairs so you can relax and communicate easily. People will open up far more readily in this kind of atmosphere. If your office isn't suitable, can you find another room which is? At the very least, move the chairs away from the desk.

The right approach

Remember that the candidates are vetting you, so try to behave as though you are on show as much as they are. Treat every candidate as though they are a potential star employee and you are only one of several organizations they are considering working for. So you need to give the best possible impression to be sure that they take the job if you offer it, even if they get four or five other offers at the same time.

Be polite and friendly, and give them a taste of the attitudes they can expect to encounter if they come to work for you. In particular, listen to them, show that you want to hear their views, ideas and opinions, and encourage them to ask questions. Demonstrate that you view communication as a two-way process that you are happy to give out information and you welcome input from everyone.

Final impressions

What about all the unsuccessful candidates? Remember, the person you reject for this job might be perfect for the next job you advertise, so you want to make the best impression you can. Write everyone a letter which will make them think 'What a shame, I'd have loved to work for that company' rather than 'Well, sod you, then.' So address the letter personally, thank them for their interest and assure them you'll keep their details on file in case a more suitable post comes up in the future. And remember, the phrase 'This job isn't the right one for you' is much less of a put down than 'You're not right for this job.'

Appraisal

Your employees' best opportunity to express their opinions, ambitions, fears, problems, positive and negative feelings about their job is at their annual appraisal interview. Which means that their appraisal is *your* best opportunity to communicate your attitude to their opinions, ambitions, fears and so on. The messages you transmit at appraisal will stay with your interviewee at least until their next appraisal in a year's time; so you'd better make sure you give the right impression.

What is an appraisal?

First of all, you have to understand exactly what an appraisal is – and what it is not. To many people, it is just an annual, or biannual, opportunity to pat your staff on the back, or to tick them off, depending on your approach. It's not worth the time it takes, but while it's company policy to hold annual appraisals you have to go through the charade.

Wrong. An appraisal is the best opportunity you will get to motivate each of your staff on a one-to-one basis. It is their annual incentive booster. But you have to recognize that the appraisal is for *their* benefit, not yours. It's their interview. And the more they get out of it, the better their performance will be afterwards – that's your pay-off.

An effective appraisal is the employee's chance to find out how well they're doing, to discuss ongoing problems and grievances, to talk about ideas and ambitions for the future, and to express their views – positive and negative – about their job. It is also their opportunity to let you know if you could help or support them more than you do; so you may have to accept some criticism.

It should be clear that none of this is going to happen unless the mood is right. You need the interviewee to be as relaxed as possible. So take all the measures we looked at earlier to create a relaxed atmosphere – an informal, comfortable seating arrangement, an unhurried tone and a friendly approach.

And one other thing: no surprises. The employee has to be sure that they are not going to be ticked off for anything. You can't relax if you suspect there may be unpleasant surprises waiting for you. So have an absolute rule that you *never* use an appraisal to discipline anyone – even if the discipline interview needs to be held on the same day; do it separately. This should also make you see that you must discuss any problems as soon as they happen throughout the year – otherwise you can't have a relaxed and easy appraisal with no surprises.

I'm not saying you can't discuss any negative aspects of the employee's performance at an appraisal – you may well need to – but you should only discuss mistakes and areas where they fail to meet standards despite genuinely trying to. These are not disciplinary problems and the employee will be expecting them to arise during the interview.

Create the right mood

Before you even begin the interview you need to set up an informal and unhurried atmosphere. Don't face the interviewee imposingly across the desk; sit at right angles to them (or thereabouts) in easy chairs around a coffee table. If your office can't accommodate this layout, you'll have to hold the appraisal somewhere else. It's alarming how constraining the barrier of a desk can be in an informal meeting, even when you're deliberately working to counteract it. You can take other steps as well to generate a relaxed mood and to give the impression that you are an approachable type of person all year round, not just at appraisal.

➤ Slip into the interview gently, with a minute or two of general chat at the start. Arrange for coffee or tea and while it's arriving ask the interviewee how they're coping with the new computer system, or how their driving test went last week. It relaxes them, and reassures them that they're not going to be disciplined instead of appraised. Of course, *you* know that appraisals aren't for disciplining, but if the interviewee is under-confident, or recently worked for a manager who did use appraisals to discipline, they may still be nervous.

➤ If you and the interviewee have a similar sense of humour, allow it to show from time to time during the appraisal. A laugh always relaxes people.

➤ Be human, and refer to your own weak points from time to time, so that they can see that you don't expect them to find everything easy. So when they tell you that they find all the figure-work they have to do quite difficult, say, 'Ah, but at least once you've worked it out, you just bang it into the computer. I'd still be there an hour later trying to work out how to get the software to do what I wanted.'

Adopt a positive attitude

Your approach to the interview communicates your commitment to the person, their job and the organization. So make sure you adopt the right attitude:

➤ *Prepare.* Thorough preparation shows that this appraisal is important for you as well as for the interviewee. Let them see that you have done your paperwork. (The companion volume in this series, *The Seven Deadly Skills of Management*, covers appraisal skills including how to prepare for the interview.)

➤ *Encourage honesty.* If you take criticism of yourself, the organization or other staff badly, the appraisee will quickly learn not to be honest. So respond positively to any kind of honesty, while making sure the employee sticks to the point so the discussion can't degenerate into a personal slagging off session about everyone the employee doesn't care for. If they start to criticize, say 'I really can't discuss this now. I think you should arrange a time when both of you can come and see me together so we can work this out.' This stops any kind of generalized moaning and really is the best solution if the complainant is serious.

> *Ask for their views.* Show the interviewee that their feelings and opinions matter, and that you value their suggestions and ideas, by asking them to tell you what they think and make notes. And ask for their view before you give yours, not only to avoid colouring their response, but also to show that their opinion has at least equal weight.

> *Quote specific examples.* Whether you are citing problem areas or achievements, give specific examples of the person's performance to show that you notice their work – good as well as bad.

> *Criticize carefully.* Appraisal shouldn't feel like a gauntlet which the interviewee has to run. Of course you need to discuss areas of weakness, but discuss the performance, not the person and do it positively, as we saw earlier. Ideally, encourage them to criticize themselves: 'So how do you feel you cope with the figurework you have to do?'

Address their concerns

You use an appraisal to ask your employees, among other things, to tell you their worries, hopes, fears and ambitions. When they do, you must respond with more than just a polite smile and the right body language. This is your opportunity to demonstrate that you are there to make your employees' contribution as effective as possible. If they could be more productive given better resources or conditions, or if certain restrictions or problems were removed, it is your job to bring these changes about if you possibly can.

At appraisal, you can communicate this commitment to your staff: if someone raises a matter at appraisal that is important to them, *do something about it*. At the very least, you can think seriously about it and arrange to discuss it again later with them, but you should take any suggestion, complaint, resentment or ambition seriously and follow it up after the interview. The best you can hope for is that your employees' commitment to the organization will equal your own – it won't better it. And they will assess your commitment by the way you deal with these issues.

Discipline interview

The very best managers almost never have to discipline anyone. The reason is simple: if you communicate effectively with your team, and motivate them thoroughly, they will work their hardest for you and there will be no cause for disciplining any of them. You may need to correct mistakes from time to time, in a positive way, but that's hardly the same thing.

It's useful for you to consider, if ever you do feel you have to take disciplinary action, where you have gone wrong; if you had done your job perfectly it wouldn't have come to this. This doesn't mean that if you have a disciplinary problem it's all your own fault, but that somewhere along the line you have almost certainly contributed to the problem, whether by action or by omission. If you don't identify *all* the causes of the problem you have less chance of preventing it happening again, so make sure you identify your own part of the cause.

Is it *really* necessary?

If you're running a successful and well-motivated department, you should think twice before you discipline anyone. A well-motivated employee who does something wrong is almost certainly doing it through genuine mistake or accident, in which case they need correcting but not disciplining. If they make a lot of mistakes with the paperwork, for example, it's more likely to be because they don't understand the new forms, or they are distracted by a serious personal problem which you know nothing about, or even that their eyesight is getting worse. None of these is a disciplinary problem, although they will need addressing.

If your team members are motivated and commited, acknowledge the fact. Talk to them when they make mistakes, make sure they realize there's a problem and discuss the reasons behind it and the lessons they can learn. But be very, very wary of disciplining them; if they are already committed you may well do more harm than good.

The interview

Having said all that, just occasionally you may still find that you have to discipline someone. When you do, there are certain guidelines to follow that will make the discipline more effective and won't damage the morale of the person concerned, or the people working around them:

1   *As soon as you are aware of the problem, tackle it immediately.* Don't wait until you're certain there's a serious disciplinary matter to deal with. There are several good reasons for this:

➤ If someone is out of line it will affect everyone else. Not only will they often be frustrated by the problem itself, they will also resent the fact that someone is getting away with something which is affecting them detrimentally. So take action before there's a chance for resentments to build up.

➤ It's much easier to deal with someone over a small, minor problem than over a persistent, major one. If they are trying it on, a swift, relatively subtle warning could be all it takes to make them see that they're not going to get away with it. The longer you leave things to run, the more unpleasant the eventual, and inevitable, interview will be for both of you.

➤ Some kinds of disruptive behaviour can become habits and be much harder to break. If someone's time-keeping starts to slip and they begin turning up later in the mornings, they may quite quickly reach the point where they find it pretty hard to get out of bed at the earlier time they used to. To give another example, a lunchtime drink which turns into several lunchtime drinks can be difficult to cut back down if you don't take action promptly.

➤ If you do nothing about a particular type of behaviour, the message you communicate is that the behaviour is OK. If you suddenly call someone in to your office weeks later and discipline them for it, it really isn't fair. If it isn't OK, let them know straight away.

2   *Confidentiality is essential.* If you discipline someone, never let anyone else (except your own boss, if necessary) know what's going on and never comment later on any disciplinary action. If you talk to one member of your department about another one, the assumption will be that you would talk as freely about them.

This deeply undermines people's trust in you and damages their confidence in being able to talk to you about their own problems or weaknesses.

3   The previous point still holds good even if you are disciplining someone following a complaint by someone else in your department or organization. Just because they made the complaint, they don't have a right to know what was said in the interview. They need to know only that you have done something about the matter and that you want to know if the problem recurs.

4   *Be consistent.* You will undermine your employees' motivation incredibly fast if you treat people differently for what is effectively the same behaviour. If you let one person arrive late every morning and do nothing about it, but you disciplined someone else last year for doing exactly the same thing, you will earn a reputation for being unfair – and rightly. The same goes if you have a quiet word with one person and issue a verbal warning to the next. Just because you have to be totally confidential about what goes on in your discipline interviews, there's no rule that says the interviewee has to. Often when they come out of your office their colleagues will be crowding round saying 'What happened?' So make sure that they all tell the same story and that you can justify any difference in their treatment.

Bad news interview

We all dislike having to break bad news, but occasionally it has to be done. Perhaps one of your team members hasn't got the promotion they applied for, or they can't have the extra staff they asked for. These interviews can be very sensitive and the way you handle them has a strong impact on the interviewee's view of both you and the organization.

You can handle most of the interview by following the communication principles in this book, but one of the trickiest things to deal with is the other person's emotion. Some people clam up completely, others lose their temper or burst into tears. Any of these reactions can be disconcerting if you're not sure how to handle it, so here are a few pointers.

The silent response

There's an argument that if someone doesn't want to talk, you shouldn't make them. That's all very well if they really don't want to, but people often clam up because they are uncomfortable about showing their emotions. Up to a point, you have to guess for yourself whether the person really doesn't want to speak, or would like to but feels they can't. You will find, however, that it helps to take their normal personality into account. Are they normally chatty and open? If so, they probably want to be able to talk about the bad news. If, on the other hand, they are naturally quiet and reserved, it's more likely that their silence is a genuine indication that there's nothing they feel the need to say. If you think that they need to be drawn out, handle it carefully.

➤ Don't decide on their behalf the gravity of the news. You may think it's a minor irritation, but to them it could be terrible. If you say 'Don't worry, it's not the end of the world' they may become even more silent, feeling that if they show their feelings you'll think they're overreacting.

➤ Make it clear that their feelings matter by showing that you've set aside plenty of time for this interview and you're concerned about their response.

➤ Encourage them to talk by asking open questions – ones which they can't answer simply with yes or no. And encourage them to ask you questions. Don't ask them 'Have you got any questions?' in case they say 'No'. Instead say, 'What questions would you like to ask?'

➤ Don't expect them to establish how they feel, or to make decisions based on the news, until they have had time for it to sink in. It's no good saying 'The bad news is that you haven't got the transfer to the Watford branch. Now, that being the case, will you be staying on here or not?' Even if there are no decisions resting on this news, arrange a time to talk again in a day or two, once they've had time to think. This will give them a chance to get over their initial shock or upset, without depriving them of the chance to ask questions or discuss the ramifications of the news.

➤ As always, don't discuss what has been said in confidence at the interview with anyone else in the organization.

The emotional response

➢ Some people find a hug very comforting when they're upset, or perhaps just a hand to hold. Others dislike physical contact at the best of times and especially when they're feeling vulnerable. While these actions should never be rehearsed, it helps to consider in advance whether your own natural response will be the best one or not if this interview becomes emotional. Take into account the nature of the bad news as well. If the interviewee holds you in some way responsible for the decision to turn down their proposal, for example (whether you do or not) they might love a hug – but not from you. Take into account your respective sexes as well.

➢ Another option is to have a third person present at the interview to comfort the interviewee if they need it. This may seem excessive if you're telling them that they can't have an extra member of staff, but if you're telling they can't have compassionate leave to look after their dying mother they may need emotional support. Since the interview is confidential you will need to be careful to choose someone appropriate, such as someone from the personnel department. Or you could start the interview without a third person, but offer to call in someone of their choice if they become upset. If they do opt for this, call their chosen colleague in as discreetly as possible; use the phone rather than opening the door and calling, or getting your secretary to call.

➢ If the interviewee clearly wants to cry but is embarrassed to do so in front of you, ask if they'd like a few minutes on their own. Go and make them a cup of tea or coffee so they can have five minutes to themselves. By the same token, when you have finished the interview, let them stay where they are until they're ready to go out and face their workmates. Make an excuse to leave the room for 20 minutes and let them know they have the time to themselves. If you really can't be out of your office for 20 minutes, hold this kind of interview somewhere else which won't be disturbed, in case this happens.

➢ Don't abandon the interview. A few people may use tears in an attempt – conscious or unconscious – to change your mind or persuade you to try to alter the situation. Be sensitive and sympathetic to their feelings, but don't be swayed from a decision which you believe is right simply because of the other person's response to the news.

Induction

Do you remember the last time you started a new job? Whether you join the organization in a very junior role, or as a middle or senior manager, it can be nerve-racking. And the younger you are, and the less experience you have of starting a new job, the more confused and nervous you are likely to be.

 Honing Your Deadly Skills **The way you communicate with new starters in the organization will colour their view of the organization for months or years, especially if it is backed up by their subsequent experiences. So it's essential you present the best impression you can.**

For a start, treat inductees as special. Circulate a note before they arrive to the people they'll be working with, with one or two snippets of information such as where they trained, or who they last worked for. When they arrive, look after them, give them star treatment, answer their questions, show them everything they need to see, lay on a special lunch for them: let them see that your employees are your most important asset and you know it – and now they're joining the group. Don't let them down with a bump on day two, but slowly change your approach to them, so that by the end of a week or two they no longer want to be treated as special – they want to be regarded as one of the team.

The same treatment, by the way, goes for temps – who often become permanent staff or important customers. If they are only with you for a day or two you obviously won't be able to invest the same amount of effort, but you should still give them the same courtesies, introduce them to the people they need to know, and allocate someone to look after them.

Day one

Make the first day very different. Schedule in some time in the afternoon to get stuck into a suitable task so they feel they are making a contribution, but mostly treat this as *their* day. Make the first day a short one – it can be very tiring for them. Start them at about 10.00 or 10.30 and make sure someone is ready to greet them as soon as they arrive. As their manager, you should expect to spend a couple of hours with them off and on throughout the day, and someone else should be detailed to spend all day looking after them. At some point they should meet at least one of the senior managers or directors – or someone a couple of steps or so up the organizational ladder – not just for a quick handshake and out again, but for a good few minutes.

Here's a rundown of the kind of things you should incorporate into the first day's schedule:

➢ *Paperwork.* You'll need to go through a few administration and safety procedures, which you should aim to do yourself.

➢ *Introductions.* After this, you can show them to their desk and introduce them to a colleague who will show them around. They need to be introduced to their immediate colleagues, shown their way around the site (with a map if necessary), and shown the loos, the canteen, the fire exit and so on. They may also need to know how the phone works and what the computer password is.

➢ *Organization briefing.* Someone, preferably someone senior, should give the new employee an outline of the organization's history, mission statement, products or services and future aims.

➢ *Work briefing.* There are plenty of basics you should discuss with your new employee, such as hours of work, monitoring, appraisal, grievance and discipline procedures, team briefing system, pay arrangements, health and safety matters and so on. This should all be put together in an employees' handbook, but you should still go through it in person as well.

➢ *Lunch.* It's a good idea, especially if the new person is going to be part of a close team, to organize a team or departmental lunch to welcome them. This makes them feel wanted and gives them a chance to meet everyone. It only needs some fancy sandwiches and a bowl of fruit in the boardroom if you can't run to any more than that – it's the principle that matters.

➤ *Productive task.* Some kind of task which is quick to explain, such as keying in data to the computer, or planning an outline schedule for an event, or writing a press release on a fairly straightforward topic, makes the person feel they have actually started the job. Allow a couple of hours or so on the first day for 'real' work like this, and give them one or two meaty tasks, not half a dozen errands no one else can be bothered with.

➤ *Debriefing.* Spend 15 or 20 minutes at the end of the day discussing how they have felt and answering any questions. Send them home half an hour or so early, and give them some reading material to take with them, such as the company report, product catalogue or press cuttings file.

Day two onwards

Have a briefing and debriefing session with the new employee at the start and end of the second day, and arrange for a colleague to take them to lunch. Other than that, get them working at the job itself, but schedule in a mid-morning and mid-afternoon session to introduce them to colleagues in other departments, or to show them round other parts of the building, or other sites, or give them a demonstration of the organization's products.

For the rest of the first week, give them either work or on-the-job training, whichever is required, but give them one session each day to acquaint themselves with other parts of the organization, or to visit customers or retail outlets or whatever applies to your company. At the end of the week, hold another debriefing session with them, answer any questions and discuss their initial training.

It will take this first week for the employee to get an idea of what they feel they need to know, and in what order, to do the job effectively. In a junior post this may involve fairly minimal on-the-job training; in a senior management role there could be a lot to do and the inductee may feel they need a lot of information or training before they can do it properly. Either way, you will need to decide together what should be done and when, and the end of the first week is a good time to sit down and agree a training programme.

Review the inductee's progress with them again at the end of the second week, then again after the first month, so that they can assess how they are doing and can ask you any questions they want to. After that, if everything seems to be running smoothly, treat them as an established employee, but aim to hold their first appraisal interview after the first three or four months.

Summary

The way you communicate with individuals in your organization has a huge impact on their motivation, morale and productivity. The key communication lessons for motivating people through everyday contact are:

Motivation

➤ say what you mean;

➤ focus on ends, not means;

➤ be positive;

➤ be likeable;

➤ be generous.

One of the key ways of communicating with individuals is through interviews, and the four main types of interview through which you can influence your staff are as folows:

Selection

➤ give a good first impression from the moment you start to advertise the vacancy;

➤ prepare for the interview thoroughly;

➤ make sure the candidates are expected and welcomed;

➤ remember that you are being interviewed by the candidate as well as the other way around;

➤ use the same good communication techniques you do with your existing employees;

➤ give a good impression even to the candidates you reject.

Appraisal

➤ the appraisal is for the employee's benefit, not yours;

➤ its function is to let the person know how they are doing;

➤ it is not the forum for disciplining or springing surprises;

➤ create a relaxed atmosphere;

➤ be positive;

➤ be committed to addressing the employee's concerns.

Discipline

➤ be sure that disciplining really is necessary;

➤ deal with issues of discipline as soon as you become aware of them;

➤ maintain confidentiality;

➤ be consistent in the way you treat people.

Bad news interviews

➤ be prepared for an emotional response;

➤ if the interviewee clams up, ask open questions;

➤ if they are likely to become upset, consider in advance how best to comfort them;

➤ don't give up on the interview, or allow the other person's tears to change your decision.

Induction

One of the most crucial times when you can use your communication skills to influence people is when they first join the organization. The way you handle their induction will influence their attitude to the organization for months or even years. Treat them as if they're special, and make sure their induction incorporates:

➢ paperwork;

➢ introductions;

➢ an organization briefing;

➢ a work briefing;

➢ lunch with colleagues;

➢ a productive task;

➢ debriefing.

Communicating Under Pressure

The people who work for you will judge you largely by the way you behave in a crisis – these will be the most memorable occasions, after all. If you fall apart when the computer goes down, or behave insensitively when an employee dies, both you personally and the organization will be branded as ineffectual or insensitive for years to come. This in turn will affect morale and productivity, and will colour the staff's view of the corporate personality.

The good news is that handling these times well can hugely improve your relationship with your staff and, as a result, their loyalty and dedication to you and the organization. This final chapter is about how to apply the lessons of good communication we have learnt in the rest of this book when they are being tested the most – under pressure.

There are certain ground rules to follow for coping under pressure, which we'll look at first. These rules apply in any crisis you encounter in either of the two main categories:

➢ accidents, such as the basement flooding or the switchboard crashing;

➢ domestic problems, such as a member of your department being sacked or someone dying.

The seven deadly skills of communicating under pressure

The key rules for communicating under pressure are all rules we have covered elsewhere for communicating at any time with your staff. They are especially important in times of stress, such as organizational mergers, redundancies, restructuring and so on. But under the kind of immediate pressure we are talking about here, they are critical and you can't afford to let any of them slip.

Honing Your Deadly Skills: **The intelligent approach to communicating under pressure is to incorporate the rules into your everyday working life so thoroughly that when you are really up against it, they come to you entirely without effort (which you won't be able to spare).**

There are seven key rules to follow when you are communicating under pressure:

1 *Keep everyone informed about what's happening all the time.* If people don't understand what is happening, that's when they make it worse. If you don't tell them, for example, that the emergency services will be here to deal with the flood in ten minutes so there's no need to take any risks, someone will make things worse by opening a door which had been holding back the flood to check whether anything on the other side needs rescuing. Obviously, keeping people informed in a domestic crisis doesn't mean breaching confidentiality. If everyone finds out that one of the team is HIV positive, you shouldn't give them any other information (if you have it yourself) unless the person involved asks you to.

2 *Get everyone together to give them important instructions or information collectively.* When everyone is working fast and some are flustered or even panicky, the last thing you need is a game of Chinese whispers. Make sure that everyone has the same information at the same time, so there's no cause for lengthy discussion or confusion. Even if no one is bailing out the basement for five minutes while you talk to them all, it will still save time in the long run. If you really feel the crisis warrants it, collect everyone in the basement and give them all a bucket while you talk to them. But only if the task is mindless – don't risk them concentrating on the job so hard that they stop listening to you.

3 *Encourage people to ask questions if they need to, even if time is at a premium.* The alternative can be far worse: not only will people

fail to understand, or get hold of the wrong end of the stick, but they will then be released into the crisis area, armed with their misinformation and faulty grasp of the facts, with an instruction to help resolve the problem.

4   *Involve people in key decisions.* The more control people have, the more committed they are. It isn't always possible to involve people fully if there is an emergency where instant action is called for, but if a member of staff has died, for example, involve their colleagues in deciding who should offer sympathy to the family and in what form, whether anyone from the organization should attend the funeral, and so on.

5   *Be available.* If any of your staff wants to talk to you, you should be there and listen to them fully. In a serious crisis this may well mean postponing appointments and meetings outside the department. But remember, your staff are under pressure too and they need you there even if you feel you can afford to leave the office for an hour or two.

6   *Let them see that you're rooting for them.* You may need to put your department's case to other departments or to senior management, to get them an extension on a project deadline, or extra resources to cope with the problem. Your staff need to know that you're out there, working for them – even fighting for them if necessary.

7   *Keep your sense of humour.* One of the best forms of stress relief is laughter and if you can get your team to laugh in a crisis (which doesn't mean easing off the work if there's a lot to do) it will have a lot of benefits. The atmosphere will be less fraught, which will help to minimize any conflict, and you will be perceived as being calm and in control. Not only that, but it eases the pressure on your staff because they can see that you're not strung out and about to snap at them, so they can relax.

So those are the seven deadly skills of communicating under pressure. Important skills at any time; crucial in an emergency. You should apply them whether one of the team has developed a serious illness, or you're all stuck in the warehouse for the weekend because you got locked in and the phones have gone down.

These kinds of pressured situations can be really good news for a team in the long run. Often there is a kind of blitz mentality which brings everyone together and reinforces the group, as members of the department or team have no option but to pull together. And a crisis can bring out qualities or skills in people that no one knew they had – a particularly calm head, a proper grasp of electrical safety, or a talent for picking locks – and their colleagues look at them in a different light afterwards.

Accidents

Fire, flood, bomb scare, blackout, a customer collapsing – these kinds of accidents are rare, but sooner or later one of them will happen. It may be something you could never have predicted, such as the board of directors trapped on the roof in a blizzard when the door jams after they've gone on a site visit to the proposed helipad. These crises tend to hit out of the blue and you often have no time to think. You have to take action fast to prevent things getting even worse.

 Honing Your Deadly Skills: **Many managers understandably rely on their own ability to think on their feet in these situations, on the grounds that there is no option. But while you do certainly need to keep a clear head and make quick decisions, there are also things you** *can* **do to prepare for this kind of emergency, even if you don't know what it's going to be.**

Have a first aider

Every working group or team should have at least one qualified first aider. Sooner or later they are likely to be called on. You need to start by working out which groups need a first aider.

➢ Each main department, broadly speaking, should have at least one first aider – sales, marketing, distribution, accounts. This means that if, for example, there is an emergency in the sales department and their first aider is at lunch, you shouldn't have to go too far to find someone else qualified to cope.

➢ Each *site* should have at least two first aiders, so it is covered even when one is on holiday (or off sick). So if the distribution department works from its own building some distance away from everyone else, they will need more than one first aider. The only exception to this is when the department or section is so small that it becomes impractical. If you have a regional sales team of five people in an office in Exeter, one first aider is likely to be enough.

➤ If a site is particularly dangerous, you will need more first aiders. If you have a large heavy engineering factory with 200 workers in it, all lifting sheet metal and using welding machines and fork-lift trucks, obviously you will need three or four qualified first aiders on the premises to be absolutely sure that there is someone available at any time.

➤ If a group of people works at irregular times, you still need a qualified first aider. It's not enough to have three first aiders in the building if they all go home at 5.30 and there's no one on the night shift trained to cope if there's an accident.

Once you've established where you need first aiders, and how many of them you should have, you need to decide who they should be.

1 Start with a list of everyone in the departments or the premises which need first aiders.

2 Now cross off everyone who is frequently off site or unavailable.

3 Next, eliminate anyone who you, or their manager, suspects might go to pieces in a crisis.

4 The remaining people on the list are all potential first aiders.

There's no point trying to force someone to train as a first aider if they don't want to. So work through the list, starting with the people you reckon would be the most cool-headed if they were called on and ask them if they would be prepared to train. Some won't want to, but you shouldn't have any trouble finding someone who would like to.

Take first-aid training seriously and let the people who take the training know that they are taking on an important and valuable responsibility, even if you do hope not to have to call on them often. I was once sent on a St John's ambulance first aid course, which as far as I recall was very good. But it was never mentioned again; I'm not sure if my employer, or any one else in the building, would even have remembered in an emergency that I was supposed to be able to help.

Then again, after about a year or so I'd forgotten most of it anyway, so it's probably a good thing they never asked me to assist. My experience – and I fear many other people's is the same – carries important lessons:

➢ Everyone should know, and be reminded from time to time, who the qualified first aiders are in case they need them.

➢ First aiders need to be given top-up training regularly so that they don't forget their training.

➢ If you ask someone to take on the responsibility of first-aid training, don't ignore their commitment. They may never be called on to practise their skills but, if they are, they could be putting themselves in line for a very traumatic experience, perhaps even one in which they hold the balance of life or death. So give them recognition for this and give them the training they need to make emergency decisions if they have to.

Plan for the most likely scenarios

You may not know what crises, if any, you may meet in future, but you can guess which you are most likely to meet, or which would matter most. So think through the key emergencies and plan the outline of what you will do in case of fire, or if someone collapses, or in any other realistic, if unlikely, situation. Some organizations, such as utility and public transport companies, know they are vulnerable to bomb threats. If you keep dangerous chemicals on site you should plan what you'd do if there is a spillage. If all your most valuable equipment or stores are in the basement, you should prepare for a flood if a water pipe bursts.

The best way to plan these things is to hold a crisis planning meeting regularly – say once a year – at which you thrash out which emergencies are worth planning for and what the plan should be. Of course you don't know where your hypothetical fire might break out, but you can decide what the procedure should be, whether there should be a central liaison person and if so who (and a deputy in case the key person is away), which buildings or parts of the building would be most at risk, whether the chemicals store should be made safe as a priority (and by whom), who should be notified outside the site, whether the site gates should be closed, and so on. Should you have different levels of emergency – it might be a bit much to evacuate the whole 15-acre site because there's a small fire in an isolated shed – and if so what, and who, decides which level you're at?

These are only a few points to give you an idea of the sort of thing that you *can* plan in advance. In every case, you must all know who is responsible and what happens if they aren't there. This kind of planning is also terribly useful because it often throws up problems no one had noticed – the fire extinguisher is on the other side of a door which is locked at 5.30 and is therefore not accessible to anyone working late. Or big company meetings are always held on the fourth floor, and there aren't enough exits for that number of people to get out quickly in an emergency.

You should review these plans once a year because otherwise everyone will have completely forgotten that you have a plan, let alone what it is, when the building finally catches fire in six years' time. Or they'll find that the key person they're supposed to contact left the organization three years ago. Plans need updating – not only do people leave but buildings change use, or new potential emergencies arise.

Once you have planned what will happen in a crisis, you need to tell everyone who might be involved. If you decide that in the event of a chemical spillage the person who discovers it should phone the emergency services immediately, you'd better tell anyone who is remotely likely to discover it. Otherwise they may call the liaison person instead, who will know the plan and assume that the person calling them has already called the emergency services. It could take precious minutes to discover that neither of them has made the critical phone call.

Everyone in your team or department who is likely to be involved in handling any kind of accident or crisis should be included in an annual crisis planning session to make sure that everyone knows and remembers what their role will be. For example, the receptionist will need to know what to do with incoming calls, how to deal with anyone waiting in reception and how to handle calls from the press. These sessions are actually very good for team morale, especially if you role play a few potential crises, and they reassure people that they are working for a professional, well-organized and prepared company.

Plan who will take what role

When you look around the people you work with, there are usually some who make you think 'If ever there's an emergency, I hope they're standing right next to me', and others who make you feel 'If there's a crisis, I hope they're out of the building that day.' Well, if you do run into trouble, you don't have to leave it so much to chance. There are certain key roles that need filling in an emergency, which you can identify and allocate in advance, so that when a crisis strikes, you know where you want everyone. Some of these roles should be discussed, and the best person to fill them chosen by the group, at your crisis planning session. Others you will want to plan for and then keep to yourself. There are eight key roles, some of which can be combined in one person if necessary, and others which need a dedicated person who isn't doing anything else at the same time. Some roles can be taken by more than one person – if you have two cool-headed people, for example, you may well be able to use them both.

1   *The 'yes' person.* In an emergency, when decisions have to be made fast, it's often a good idea to have someone by your side who agrees without arguing. There is a time for saying 'Wouldn't it be better if we moved the computers first?' and the middle of a crisis isn't it. Frequently, in an emergency, it doesn't matter much (within reason) what decision you make, so long as you make it fast and with conviction. It's a good idea to identify someone to whom you will say 'I need you here with me', because you know they will set a good example by doing whatever you tell them without trying to debate it first.

2   *The cool headed person.* Many emergencies call for someone with a clear head in a crisis. They may or may not be good at decision making; if not, you can tell them what to do. But this is the first aider, or the person who evacuates the building because they'll remember to check the loos as well as the offices, or the one who calls the ambulance because they won't go to pieces and forget the address. This is a role for which the department can propose someone at a crisis planning session; that way you know they'll have the support of their colleagues.

3   *The decision maker.* Here's another role that the team can help appoint, because it has to be someone they all respect. They may be senior, or they may simply be someone with natural author-

ity – it doesn't matter. Many emergencies happen in two places at once and you need someone to be in charge in the place you can't be; someone able to make decisions and cope well in your place. For example, if you have a fire, one person needs to deal with the fire and empty the building, while someone else is checking and counting people at the muster point in the car park.

4   *The panicker.* This is the person you're trying to get rid of (this is a role to identify and keep to yourself). At best they will get in the way, at worst they will panic everyone else. You clearly can't tell them to leave or they'll be gutted, so you need to find them a job which gets them out of the way. For example, 'Jake, once we've cleared up the worst of the damage we need to box up all the undamaged stock as soon as possible. Can you take care of it? You'll need to go and round up as many boxes as you can, and then go and buy some packing tape.'

5   *The gregarious one.* Another one for the team to choose – you often need to ask for outside help in a crisis. If your exhibition stand collapses overnight, someone has to go round the other exhibitors asking for a spare chair or a couple of light bulbs. If there's a burst water pipe, someone has to persuade the emergency plumber to come out in the next half hour. Some people have a natural talent for encouraging others to help and this can be a valuable quality in a crisis.

6   *The genius for detail.* This is often your secretary, PA or assistant, but it may not be. You need someone who knows it is their job to think of all the things you might have forgotten. They need to be able to limit themselves to important points, so pick someone who isn't going to harp on minor details. You need someone who says things like 'If you bring down the spare exhibition stand from head office, it will be too short to take the new display boards' or 'We can't turn off the electricity at the mains because we won't be able to get at the fuse boxes.'

7   *The problem solver.* Sometimes you can get hung up on one particular problem which is difficult to solve. Give it to the problem solver, and an assistant if they need one, while you get on with everything else. For example, how are you going to get this expensive and vital piece of equipment out through the

door and away before the rising water level reaches it? This is another good job for the team to allocate.

8   *The sympathizer.* Some people have the gift of distributing tea and sympathy to evacuated customers or injured workers. If this is needed, don't waste a natural sympathizer on jobs anyone can do. It is a skilled role and, again, your staff can tell you who they think would be best for this role.

Whatever the crisis, the better prepared everyone is to deal with it, and the clearer they are about their roles, the faster and more effectively it will be resolved. A minor crisis, or a major one averted just in time, may be put right by a couple of clear-headed people. But a big crisis can take a lot of people to put right. If you leave out a few people they are likely to feel they aren't wanted or needed, so if you've involved most people, find a job for the rest as well, so they feel they've helped.

It is important that if everyone throws themselves into the breach you give all of them credit for it later; don't run a post-mortem and tell people they made the wrong decision. They did the best they could in the circumstances. If it's never going to happen again, keep your opinion to yourself. If you think a decision was bad and really *has* to be discussed because it could happen again, or the principle might apply in another crisis, be very diplomatic. For example: 'I thought you made absolutely the right decision to evacuate reception. It made me wonder, with hindsight, whether it would be better another time to play down the reason for the evacuation when we ask customers to leave the building. What do you think?'

When you have time to draw breath

Some crises are less urgent than others; you count the critical time in hours rather than minutes, or minutes rather than seconds – for example a switchboard crash, however serious its results, doesn't call for the same split-second response that a major fire does. Other crises slow after a while to a manageable speed: for example, you may have to race against time to stop a flood, but the clean-up operation can happen at less of a breakneck pace.

If you have time to think, it's advisable to take advantage of it. But you won't have a lot of thinking time, so use it wisely. Don't rush headlong into the problem if you can spare five or ten minutes to find a way of approaching it more effectively.

Consider whether someone else could handle the crisis better than you. Suppose you're the marketing director and your computer goes down and therefore isn't telling you what orders are due to be dispatched today. It may be that the computer manager, sales manager or dispatch manager is in a better position than you to handle the problem. In this case, delegate – your most important job is to decide which one of them to put in charge. Don't abdicate from the problem – be around if they need you – but leave them to make the decisions. If the emergency calls for all hands on deck you could help out with everyone else and let your appointed 'crisis manager' tell you what to do. If you're going to take this role, though (and it is sometimes the best course), don't undermine them – you invested them with the authority, so now respect it.

Assuming you maintain control, and you do have a little time which you need to spend as carefully as possible, these are the guidelines to follow:

➤ *Define the problem.* What, precisely, is the problem? Take a moment to get a clear focus on what the nature of the crisis is. It isn't that the computer has gone down, it is that you can't dispatch orders on time. That is therefore the immediate problem to deal with – identifying the orders you need to send out – so it is better to focus on a temporary solution to this first and worry about the computer later.

➤ *Prioritize the parts of the problem.* Suppose you have lost several computer functions – identifying the orders, selecting the stock, issuing the dispatch notes and so on. Decide which of these matters most, so that if your resources are limited you solve the most important aspects of the problem first.

➤ *Brainstorm the options.* What can you do? Can you find out who the customers are and phone them to explain and ask what they ordered? Can you send everything out by a faster and more expensive delivery system tomorrow? Get everyone involved in this brainstorming session, which only needs to last two or three minutes if that's all you've got. Often in these situations you find it's the most junior staff who have the bright ideas, so don't just hold secret meetings with your senior managers.

➤ *Take only the decisions you need to.* Don't waste time deciding what you'll do if. . . . You haven't time. Fix a review time and leave it at that. So you might decide that, for now, you'll fix the computer and dispatch everything by emergency courier tomorrow. And you can tell everyone that you'll review that decision after the computer engineers have been. There's no point in wasting time you haven't got making decisions beyond that. The engineers might say that the computer will be down for two days. On the other hand, they may tell you at 11.00 am that they'll have it fixed by lunchtime. So concentrate on the decisions that won't wait.

➤ *Allocate tasks.* You've identified the problem, prioritized the solution, and established the options. Now it's time to allocate tasks to everyone, following the team role guidelines we just looked at.

➤ *Make sure everyone understands clearly.* If you have a minute or two still in hand, use it to make sure everyone understands the crucial points and knows what they are supposed to be doing. They are under pressure too, don't forget.

Domestic problems

The second category of crisis you are likely to encounter sooner or later is to do with people rather than events. For this reason, you need to pay close attention to how you communicate with people, since emotions may be raw. The seven key lessons for communicating under pressure apply here, but some situations are worth looking at individually because there are specific guidelines to follow.

Death and serious illness

The way you handle this is terribly important to your team, who will be shocked even if the person concerned was not close to them and may also be deeply saddened at the loss or illness of a close friend. You will probably be shocked, too and your staff will understand this. They will forgive minor mistakes so long as they can see that your heart is in the right place. That is what you have to demonstrate.

➤ As soon as you hear the news, call everyone together and tell them all at once.

➤ Be ready for some people to be seriously upset; have a company counsellor or doctor on hand if there is one. Give close colleagues time off, especially following the death of a fellow employee. Be generous (but not excessive) with this time; people need to see that you put people before profit.

➤ Following a death, give colleagues time off for the funeral and attend it yourself (unless there's a reason why this is inappropriate). Make sure the organization sends flowers, regardless of whether or not the individuals within the organization choose to do so too.

➤ Give people time to get back to normal after the tragedy and don't make it a taboo subject.

➤ If you realize you have handled things badly, say so: 'I'm sorry I didn't give all of you time off for the funeral. We were all very shaken, and I didn't see things as clearly as I should have; I can see now that we should all have been there.'

➤ If one of your staff tells you they are seriously ill, let them choose how to handle the news. They may want to keep it quiet, or they may want to tell people themselves, either individually or collectively. Be prepared, if they want it, to tell everyone yourself.

HIV

HIV is a very touchy subject with many people – and I'm not talking about the ones who are diagnosed HIV+, who need a great deal of support both inside and outside work. You are not qualified to give them all the support they need – and they doubtless won't ask you to – but one of the biggest problems for HIV+ people at work is the attitude of their colleagues and this is something you can influence. Many HIV+ people will successfully keep the fact private. If you find out you should, of course, maintain strict confidentiality. But sometimes the information leaks out, or in some cases people prefer to be open with their colleagues.

➤ People will follow your lead, so make sure you treat the HIV+ person in the same way as you did before you learned of their condition. Maintain the same level of physical contact as before; don't avoid contact, but don't keep touching them just to prove something. Unless they develop AIDS they don't need special concessions or lower standards than everyone else; this would simply be patronizing. Even if they do develop AIDS, let *them* tell *you* if they need you to make allowances. You simply need to make sure you are approachable so they can talk to you if they need to.

➢ If any of their colleagues is unhappy about working with someone who is HIV+, talk to them in private. Let them express how they feel and reassure them that their fears are groundless. Give them some literature or recommend they talk to their doctor.

➢ If the HIV+ person agrees, hold an HIV and AIDS awareness session for everyone who works with them. They may like to talk about it, or you could invite an outside expert to come and talk about it. Fear of HIV and AIDS comes from ignorance, so remove the ignorance.

➢ Once everyone has talked through their feelings and been given all the information they should need, it should become a disciplinable offence to show prejudice towards the person who is HIV+. You cannot hope to remove everyone's private prejudices, but you can make it clear that any public display of prejudice is forbidden. Take the feelings of the person with HIV into account, however. If you keep disciplining other people on their account they may start to feel uncomfortable. If the situation becomes serious, ask them how they would like you to handle it. You don't have to take their advice, but you should listen to their view before you take any decisions.

Sacking a member of the team

Sacking someone is always unpleasant and after it's done you still have to break the news to the rest of the department. This can put a lot of pressure on you, especially if the person was popular, so you need to communicate effectively with your team to ensure a supportive response.

➢ After the person has gone, talk to everyone else collectively. Don't give away anything confidential about the reasons for the dismissal, but say that you regret that it was necessary.

➤ Explain that you felt you had to dismiss the person because their presence was disruptive to the department and its members, and was inhibiting other people's ability to do their job effectively. Say you are confident that you have acted in the department's best interests.

➤ If you have acted fairly, your staff will see this, even if they are reluctant to admit it openly. They aren't daft and they know that sometimes you have no alternative but to dismiss.

Theft

The suspicion of theft by someone in the department causes a thoroughly uncomfortable and uneasy atmosphere. Everyone fears that they may be thought guilty and secretly wonders who it could be. If it is suspected that someone in your department may be guilty of theft, handle it very carefully or you could lose the loyalty of your team.

➤ It's not your job to identify the culprit; that is what the police are for. Be vigilant, and pass on to the police any information you think may be important, but don't check up on people or rummage through their filing cabinets when they're out. They will know.

➤ Your attitude must be that you are confident that no one in your team would steal from their colleagues or the organization. Therefore you will all be careful, but you won't let it interfere with your work.

➤ Don't let anyone think that you could possibly suspect them. Otherwise, when the culprit is finally identified, everyone else will have to go on working with you knowing that you thought they might be capable of theft. If you only suspected a couple of people, your relationship with them will be even worse.

Collective failure

Failure on the part of the team or department as a whole is a difficult situation to handle and one which needs all your communication skills. Maybe you've lost a big contract because you weren't as good as the next company, or poor safety standards on the part of your department have caused a serious injury.

➤ Be open, and admit that you have all failed, yourself included. 'We failed.' Let them see that as their manager, you recognize that you carry the greatest share of responsibility.

➤ Let the team see that, like all good leaders, you are taking the blame yourself as far as senior management are concerned.

➤ Hold a meeting with everyone to analyse where you went wrong. Take a positive stance: you've got the best lesson of all – failure – to learn from. So once you understand your mistakes you should be better than anyone else next time.

➤ Finish the meeting on a positive note. Nothing is all bad – get the team to identify and recognize the things they got right, so they get used again.

➤ After a day or so, start to make the occasional joke about the failure. The point of this is to show that you may have failed, but it isn't the end of the world. You need to lighten the mood and ease some of the pressure, or the team will be so demoralized that it won't have a chance of succeeding at anything else. However, don't joke about death or serious injury and don't make jokes which make any single member of the team the butt (except yourself). Don't joke about what a dreadful team you are either.

Summary

When you have an accident, an emergency, a crisis or a domestic problem in the department to deal with, remember the seven deadly skills of communicating under pressure:

1   keep everyone informed about what's happening all the time;

2   get everyone together to give them important instructions or information collectively;

3   encourage people to ask questions;

4   involve people in key decisions;

5   be available;

6   let them see that you're rooting for them;

7   keep your sense of humour.

Index